THE HORSHAM CALENDAR

OF CRIMES AND CRIMINALS

Accounts of some of the criminal cases of which there are
records in the Horsham Museum Archives

extracted by Audrey Goffe, Norman Hewell, John Hurd and
Sheila Stevens

edited by Susan C. Djabri

Published by
Horsham Museum Society

Printed by
West Sussex County Council Print Unit

ISBN 1 902484 21 5

Horsham Museum Society, founded in 1893, began to collect and display "objects of interest", some of which are still part of the collections of Horsham Museum. It also began to collect books for its Library, undertake research and publish books about local history. In 1966, Horsham District Council took over the running of the Museum from the Society and since then, professional curators have been appointed.   Horsham Museum Society continues to be actively concerned with the support of the Museum, in all aspects of its work, and maintains its Members' Library, which has a specialised collection of books on Sussex and the local history of Horsham and District. The Society holds lectures, excursions and social activities throughout the year. It also runs a local history group and an antiques and collectors' circle.   Please contact the **Honorary Secretary** at the address below for further information.

Horsham Museum Society, c/o Horsham Museum
9 The Causeway,
HORSHAM,
West Sussex RH12 1HE

Table of Contents

ACKNOWLEDGMENTS

I would like to thank Audrey Goffe, Norman Hewell, John Hurd and Sheila Stevens for all their hard work on the documents; Jeremy Knight, Curator of Horsham Museum, for launching this project, and giving us his support; and Pauline Carter for her help in organising the schedule of work and looking after the transcribers.

Susan C. Djabri

A Horsham Gaol Calendar for the Spring Assizes - March 1801

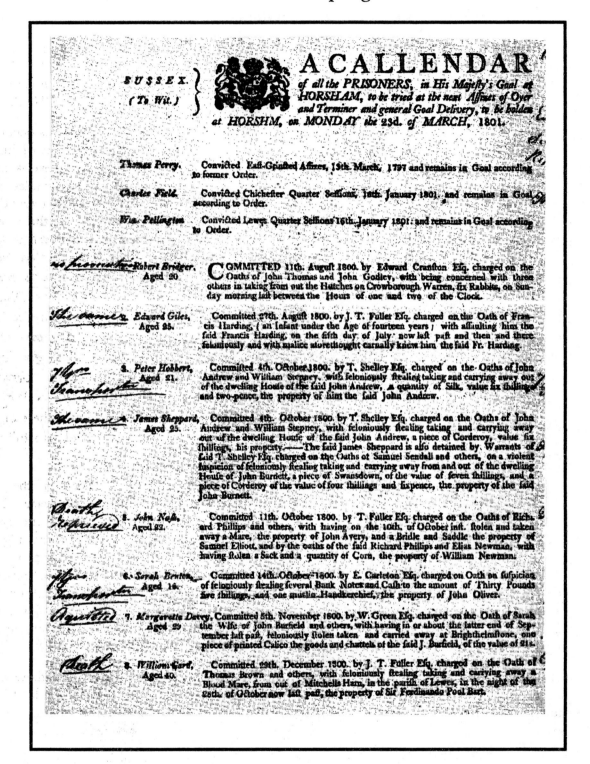

This shows the first page of a list of cases to be held at the Horsham Assizes in March 1801. It is interesting to note that some of the prisoners were committed for trial by Timothy Shelley of Field Place, father of Percy Bysshe Shelley, in his capacity as a Horsham magistrate. One case concerns the stealing of a blood mare from Sir Ferdinando Poole of Lewes, former High Sheriff of Sussex and a well-known racehorse owner, for which it is noted that the thief was sentenced to death. (Horsham Museum MSS Cat. No. 290).

✂ Introduction ✃

This booklet contains details of more than 30 interesting criminal cases, which were extracted from documents in the Horsham Museum archives by members of the Local History Group of Horsham Museum Society as their project for 2002. This project was linked with the opening of the *Crime and Punishment Gallery* in Horsham Museum on 10 May 2002, during the first national Local History Week.

In reading this booklet, it should be borne in mind that at the time most of these cases occurred, there was no professional police force, or Crown Prosecution Service. The administration of justice depended on the apprehension of suspected criminals by local parish constables, who undertook these unpaid duties in addition to their normal working life. The rules for the office of constables were originally written in 1610 by Sir Francis Bacon, but during successive editions of *The Compleat Parish Oficer* during the 18th century, it appears that their responsibilities grew with each new statute. In the seventh edition published in 1734, there is a long section on "Constables at large" . Their main duty was to keep the peace and arrest criminals, but it also said *"their duty in particular is to be considered under the Heads following, etc., Affrays, Alehouses, Arms, Arrests, Artificers, Bakers, Bastardy, Bawdy-Houses, Bridges, Butter, Buttons, Carriages, Cattle, Clothiers, Coals, Conventicles, Customs, Deer-stealing, Deserters, Distillers, Distress, Drunkenness, Dyers, Escapes, Excise, Felons, Fish, Forcible Entry, Foreign Goods, Forestallers, Game, Gaming, Gaol and Gaolers, Gunpowder, Hawkers, Hay-market, Hedge-breakers, Highways, Horses, Hue and Cry, Inns, Juries, Labourers, Land-Tax, Maltsters, Measures, Militia, Night walkers, Orchards robbed, Physicians, Plague, Popish Recusants, Post-Letters, Presentments, Prisons, Prisoners, Riots, Rogues, Robbery, Sabbath, Servants, Shoemakers, Soldiers, Supersedeas, Swearing, Taylors, Tithes, Tobacco, Vagrants, Watch, Warrants, Weights, Wrecks etc".* [1] The constables mentioned in some of these cases can be seen tackling a few of these duties, as best they could, but it was nearly another century before a professional police service, with full-time officers, came into being.

In the 18th century, the legal system further depended very heavily on the work of the local magistrates, who were also unpaid but were given the prestigious title of Justices of the Peace. They conducted the original investigation of the matter and committed the suspected prisoners for trial at the next Assizes. By the end of the 18th century, most of the local magistrates had had some legal training and took their responsibilities seriously. One can only suppose that this system worked reasonably well because, in a country town like Horsham, or in the surrounding villages, there was a sense of community and inter-dependence. Habitual petty thieves soon became well-known, and were much disliked by their neighbours. The criminals were generally opportunistic amateurs rather than hardened professionals - as can be seen in the case of the horse thief who made the mistake of stealing a horse from his aunt, and of wearing clothes which could be easily recognised!

It is clear, however, that a more professional approach was needed by the 1830s when there was a much greater threat of social breakdown. The growing agricultural poverty and distress led to disturbances throughout the south of England in the winter of 1829-1830, which are known as the "Captain Swing" riots, and these were put down very firmly by the government, who feared that revolution was about to break out. They directed the local magistrates to pass harsh sentences, and at the !830 Winter Assizes in Lewes, two men, Edmund Bushby and William Goodman, were sentenced to death for firing a hayrick, after a trial that caused controversy. William Cobbett, the radical writer, claimed that Francis Scawen Blunt and Henry Tredcroft, two of the Horsham magistrates, had forced Goodman to sign a confession; Thomas Sanctuary of Rusper, a local magistrate, who currently held the office of High Sheriff of Sussex, went to Brighton to appeal to King William IV to spare the lives of the two men. Goodman was spared, but transported for life; Bushby was executed at Horsham on 1st January 1831 before a crowd of one thousand people, most of them labourers who clearly sympathised with him. [2]

---

[1]   *The Compleat Parish Officer, 7th Edition, 1734,* republished in 1996 by Wiltshire Family History Society.
[2]   William Albery, *A Millennium of Facts in the History of Horsham and Sussex, 947-1947,* Horsham Museum Society, 1947, p. 565.

Horsham's first full-time policeman, John Coppard Gower, was appointed in 1839, and figures in some of the later cases in this booklet as a hard-working and energetic officer. But the new police force was only part of a growing professionalism of approach throughout the justice system, which was clearly necessary to keep abreast of the growing volume of work. Much of the actual organisation of the Assizes was done by the Clerk of the Peace for Sussex, an important office long held by a well-trained, professional lawyer. William Ellis of Horsham held this office from about 1774 until the early years of the 19th century, and we know from the letters that he wrote as Steward of Hills, to Lord and Lady Irwin, that he was extremely competent. The Gaol Calendar reproduced on a previous page shows something of the work he would have done in preparation for the 1801 Spring Assize Week. By the 1830s, William Stedman was clerk to the Horsham magistrates, organising their schedule of work and keeping their records.

The Sussex Assizes were held twice a year during the 18th century, in Spring and Summer. In 1800, it was decreed that the Assizes should be held alternately in Horsham and Lewes - the Summer Assizes were generally held in Horsham. A additional Winter Assizes was added later. The Quarter Sessions were held in Midhurst, Chichester and Petworth as well as Horsham, in West Sussex, from 1722 to 1800. Both civil and criminal cases were heard at the Assizes and the Quarter Session, but the Quarter Sessions were also concerned with the civil administration of the County, until the setting up of County Councils in 1888. The graver cases, concerning treason, murder, forgery, perjury, bigamy and abduction, could only be adjudicated and punished by the Judges of the Assize Court. The Assizes were presided over by Judges on circuit, who were welcomed into the town with great solemnity by the High Sheriff of Sussex in a horse-drawn coach, accompanied by a troop of young men on horseback carrying javelins. During the late 18th century, the Assizes were held at the Market Hall, which stood on the site of the present Town Hall. It was an arcaded building, which provided cover for the farmers' wives who brought their butter and cheese to Horsham on market days. During the Assizes, the lower part was boarded up to make a court room, but complaints about the draughtiness and discomfort of the venue led the Duke of Norfolk, as Lord of the Manor and Borough of Horsham, to pay for the Market Hall to be enlarged and improved in 1812, to prevent the Assizes being moved elsewhere in Sussex. This would have meant a great loss of business to Horsham, because the Assizes brought many people into the town. The new Town Hall was hailed as being "greatly superior" to any other Court of Justice in Sussex, but still could not really compare with Lewes' fine County Hall, built in 1808.

Horsham was the home of the Sussex County Gaol from 1580 until 1845, but the main responsibility of the county Gaoler was to hold the suspected criminals who had been arrested, and produce them at the Assizes - punishment took place at a "house of correction", which was a separate institution. At this time, imprisonment was not used so much as a punishment as it is now, since many more crimes were capital offences, and transportation was used as another alternative for those convicted of serious crimes. Criminals convicted of a capital offence, such as murder or robbing a mail coach, were executed immediately after trial, in a nearby public place, so Horsham was the place of execution for those sentenced to death at the Horsham Assizes. During the 18th century, executions were carried out on Horsham Common, first near Champion's windmill (off what is now King's Road) and later at the end of Brighton Road, in what is now Sandeman Way, near St. Leonard's Arms. The prisoner was brought to the gallows in a cart, the noose was put round his neck and the cart moved away. In 1820, after a badly bungled execution in which the rope was not the right length, it was decided to erect a gallows with the new "movable drop", which had already been installed at Newgate, outside Horsham Gaol in East Street. From then on, executions furnished an excuse for the notorious "Hanging Fairs" which drew in spectators and customers from much of the surrounding countryside, to view public executions on the "Horsham drop". The last such execution was that of John Lawrence for the murder of the superintendent of the Brighton Police, which took place on 6th April 1844 - it is described in detail in Henry Burstow's *Reminiscences of Horsham,* published in 1911(the book was actually written by William Albery).

In this booklet, we have sought to draw out the details of about 30 hitherto unpublished criminal cases, most of them handled by Thomas Charles Medwin or his son Pilfold, which survive among the large collection of briefs for court-cases in the Horsham Museum archives. This collection is considered to be the most important feature of the Medwin papers in Horsham Museum - few other such collections have survived elsewhere. (Even in the Public Record Office, the records of the Assize Courts have large gaps and are notoriously difficult to use). As local solicitors, it was the duty of the Medwins to find the witnesses, collect the evidence and prepare the briefs which would be presented in court by the London barrister chosen to make the case for the prosecution, or the defence, of the prisoner. It is clear that the solicitor's zeal and commitment were often the deciding factor in making the case, or obtaining the release of the prisoner, if unjustly charged. Quite apart from the Medwins' evident skill in preparing the briefs, their investigations, listing names and places, taking witness statements, and going into great detail as to what actually happened, give an unparalleled picture of life as it was actually lived in Horsham, in the late 18th and early 19th centuries, and of the way that people actually thought and spoke. It is this "fly on the wall" aspect which make these cases of such interest today, and why it was thought worth making them more easily accessible.

The actual "briefs" are large and unwieldy documents, usually several pages closely hand-written in very long lines, where it is very easy to lose one's place, in what is often repetitive and turgid legal language. The members of the Local History Group who have worked on this project have tackled their task in different ways, as each one thought best. While some passages lend themselves to being quoted more or less verbatim, and contain remarks which need to be reproduced exactly as written, in other cases it was necessary to précis the information to make it more manageable and to tell the story without going into too much repetitive or boring detail. It is for this reason that the term "extracted" has been used, rather then "transcribed", which implies a word for word reproduction of the document in question. In some cases the "briefs" are accompanied by a bundle of other documents, which may include the original notes from which the brief was written up, or bills and receipts, some of which may have been included where they are of interest. In the final editing, footnotes or comments have been added to clarify some points, or draw attention to other documents in the archive, which may add to the story. But it should be underlined that anyone seriously interested in any of these cases should always refer back to the original documents - this booklet is designed simply to give an idea of the range of information that is contained in these large bundles of papers, and make it more easily available to family and local historians. A detailed index, containing the names of the people mentioned in these cases, whether as criminals, victims, witnesses or magistrates, has also been drawn up. This gives name, occupation and place of residence, where possible, as well as catalogue number, chapter and date of case. The period from about 1775 to 1840, covered by these cases, is one for which personal information is generally hard to come by, as it precedes the first Horsham Census of 1841.

The cases in this booklet cover a wide range of crimes - arranged in chapters according to the crime (e.g. rape or murder) but it will be seen that the great majority are for theft or assault, often fuelled by drink, rather than anything more serious or criminal in intent. Even the administration of "Spanish Fly" in a hot posset of gin and beer was probably just a practical joke rather than anything more sinister! Some cases show a harshness and an insistence on the sanctity of property which may shock us today - a sixteen year old boy was sentenced to be transported for seven years for the theft of three sixpences. However, there are signs of a more humane attitude in the case of a girl, clearly suffering from post-natal depression to the point of attempting suicide, whose knife attack on her mother was not seen as malicious, and was sought to be excused by her lawyers when the matter came to trial. We are introduced to some amusing characters - an innkeeper, highly affronted at having been pilloried for allowing two French prisoners to escape, while engaged in his normal clandestine activities with the local smugglers! Also a couple of tramps, who went round the country with the rather odd habit of stealing coppers out of brewhouses! Some petty criminals, like the Stenning brothers of Wisborough Green, feature in several cases, and it seems that they were felt to be a thorough nuisance and given the title "the terror of the neighbourhood" long before a similar title came to be applied to the Shipley Gang in 1817. There are two nicely differentiated cases of rape (or attempted rape) - in one of which the girl fought her attacker off most strenuously, while in the other she seems to have been very easily persuaded! There are three cases of murder or manslaughter, but in each case it is clear that death was unpremeditated and the charge was reduced to take this into account. In fact, there is only one clear case of premeditated murder known to have taken place in Horsham, by someone in their right mind, and that was much earlier in the 18th century. John Whale, who lived at Corsletts in Broadbridge Heath, was poisoned by his wife Ann and her cousin Sarah Pledge with a dish of arsenic-laced hasty pudding in 1752. This particular case became the subject of a popular broadsheet and has already been fully covered by William Albery in *A Millennium of Facts about the History of Horsham and Suseex, 947-1947,* and by Jeremy Knight in *Horsham, Her Story - Brief Lives of Horsham Women 1200-2000 AD,* so it is not repeated here. Here the case concerning the death of Edward Smith, at the Queen's Head Inn, originally told by Henry Burstow in his *Reminiscences of Horsham,* is included because Horsham Museum has recently acquired a broadsheet, printed by the "Cheap and Expeditious Press" which sheds a certain amount of new light on this story.

A special study has also been made of several cases concerning William Cooper, former servant to Thomas Charles Medwin, and later landlord of the Green Dragon in the Bishopric, which is included as an appendix. Though the only criminal case in which he was involved was that in which he accused Dendy Napper of Warnham of beating him up in the *King's Head* in Slinfold - and he was the victim rather than the perpetrator - the papers relating to his civil cases, all conducted by his old master, the Horsham lawyer, Thomas Charles Medwin, provide us with a very substantial picture of William's life and background, and it seemed better to consider them all together, as a whole. In William's case, there is a real chance to study his "life and adventures" - to borrow a phrase used in one of the first histories of criminals produced for a public avid to read all about them - and later exemplified by the famous *Newgate Calendar,* which is the inspiration of this book.

Literature relating to crime is nothing new - it has a long history, which is not just inspired by a taste for sensationalism - it can be argued that the stories of violent crimes show up the fault lines of society in general, and therefore an interest in crime is morally defensible. In 1719, Captain Alexander Smith produced his *Compleat History of the Lives and Robberies of the Most Notorious Highwaymen, Foot-Pads, Shop-Lifts and Cheats,* which was followed by in 1734 by Captain Charles Johnson's *General History of the Lives and Adventures of the most famous Highwaymen, Murderers, Street-Robbers and Account of the Voyages and Plunders of the Most Notorious Pyrates.* These were followed by *The Tyburn Chronicle* of 1768 and the first *Newgate Calendar,* published in 1773 in 5 volumes, which recorded the histories of notorious criminals from 1700 to that date, imprisoned in Newgate Gaol. Works of literature inspired by the *Newgate Calendars* include Henry Fielding's *Jonathan Wild* and William Godwin's *Caleb Williams,* and the romantic novels of W.H. Ainsworth. (One of Ainsworth's novels, *Rookwood,* is thought to have used Cuckfield Park, which figures in one of the cases in this booklet, as its setting).

Most of the prisoners accused in the cases in this booklet would have had more than a nodding acquaintance with the cells of Horsham Gaol - they are likely to have spent some time there before they came to trial, though some were also held in the Petworth House of Correction, or sent there for later punishment. They were on the whole fortunate to find themselves in the new "model" Horsham Gaol, which had been built on a new site in East Street between 1775 and 1779, after a devastating report had been presented to the House of Commons by the great prison reformer, John Howard on the appalling state of the previous Gaol, which was on the north side of the Carfax. He found it to be filthy, plague ridden and unsafe, and is even said to have prevented a prison break-out during his visit there. The new Horsham Gaol was the first in the world to have individual cells, and was the model for many others throughout the world; the Petworth House of Correction was built on similar lines a few years later. Debtor prisoners and felons were kept apart and imprisoned in separate parts of the Gaol, with separate yards for exercise. (Debtor prisoners were subjected to a Catch 22 situation - they were imprisoned for being in debt but were thus deprived of the opportunity to work to earn enough money to pay them off - and sank ever deeper into debt the longer they remained in prison. Eventually the stupidity of this situation was recognised and legislation was brought in to help "poor debtors", but not before some had spent many years in gaol. Their cases were heard in the Court of King's Bench, rather than the Assizes or Quarter Sessions).

The four drawings of Horsham Gaol, commissioned with great foresight by Henry Michell, the brewer in 1845, at the time of its demolition, are now able to be on permanent display in the new *Crime and*

Punishment Gallery in Horsham Museum. Henry Michell said in his diary (edited by Kenneth Neale and published under the title *Victorian Horsham* in 1975) that *"Thinking that the character of the structure of the Gaol might some future day be matter for speculation by natives yet unborn, I had several sketches taken of it by Mr. Thomas Honeywood".* Henry Michell also recorded in his diary that he threw the Gaol open to public view in November 1845, during St. Leonard's Fair, and *"thousands of people flocked to see it (there were very few, even in the town of Horsham, who had ever gone over it) ...I was called upon to give my personal attendance .. and also to reiterate an explanation of the different parts of the building and the purpose to which each was applied, from the 'condemned cell' to the muederers' grave".* This booklet gives us the opportunity to publish the very striking (and modern-looking) isometric view of the Gaol in a large format, with a key, so that the detail can be better appreciated. (It should be noted however that the hard labour machine which is shown in the view was never actually built in Horsham, though there was one at Petworth). This view was previously published by William Albery in the *Millennium,* but as this book, with all his pioneering work on crime and punishment in Sussex, is not widely available, it was thought worth reprinting it here. Dr. Annabelle Hughes has recently written two articles on the history of the Sussex County Gaols, which were published in issues 4 and 5 of *Horsham Heritage,* containing her more recent research on this subject.

We have also tried to bring the stories to life with carefully chosen contemporary illustrations These are mainly drawn from W.H. Pyne's *Microcosm,* first published between 1800 and 1807, and *Etchings of Rustic Figures,* produced as an aid to artists for "the embellishment of landscape". In the years before photography, these drawings are an invaluable record of rural and industrial life in the early years of the 19th century. There are also engravings by Thomas Bewick, or the work of artists such as George Cruikshank, William Geikie, and Thomas Rowlandson who drew ordinary people in everyday situations, with varying degrees of satire. Other illustrations are drawn from broadsheets or chapbooks, early local histories, and the archives of Horsham Museum - a list of sources is given at the end of the book.

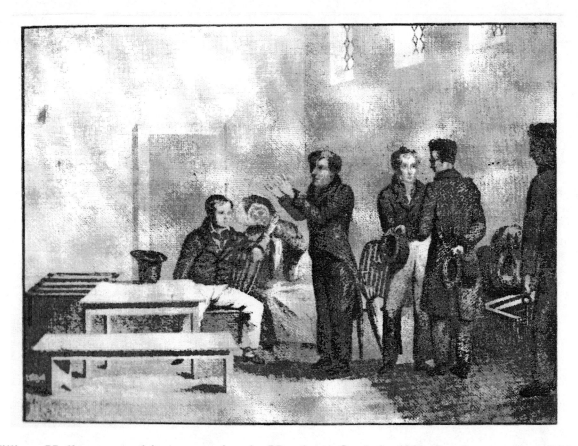

William Holloway awaiting execution in Horsham Gaol, in 1831, for the murder of his wife from William Albery's *Millennium.* This is the only known picture of a criminal inside Horsham Gaol. Though Albery says that it shows the condemned cell, it is now known to be a view of the infirmary

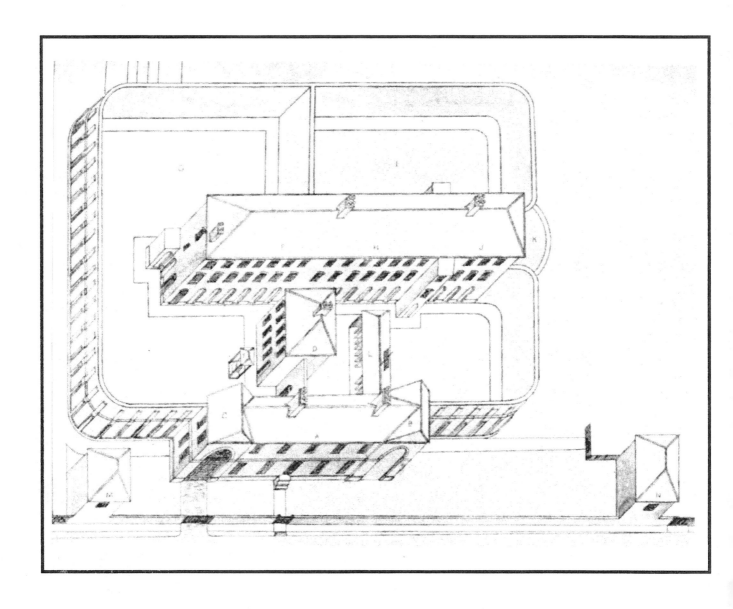

**Isometric drawing of Horsham Gaol by Thomas Honeywood,
commissioned in 1845 by Henry Michell**

Key to the drawing

A - Governor's House

B - Chapel

C - Gateway

D - Infirmary

E - Well House

F - Debtors' Prison

G - Debtors' Yard

H - Felons' Prison

I - Felons' Yard

J - Female Felons'
Prison

K - Female Felons'
Yard

L - Hard Labour
Machine

M - Coal Store

N - Stables and yard

(Note - the hard labour machine was never actually built at Horsham)

℘ Chapter One - Assault ℘

Horsham Museum MSS Cat. No. 354, *extracted by Norman Hewell.*

The King vs John Tyler, William Tyler and James Chapman Junior, for Assault on William Markbee

Michaelmas Sessions at Petworth 1790

The case for the prosecution

William Markbee had farmed for many years on a large farm at Rusper known as Gatwick Farm. His lease had run out, but under the terms of the lease, he had permission to use the barns and fodder his cattle until May Day. On 5th April 1790, he went down to the lower barn to fodder some cattle which he had there and he noticed that the penstock *(sluice)* of the barn pond had been raised thus allowing the water to flow and the force of this had caused the bank of the bay, which was used to water the cattle, to burst. He then heard voices at the upper pond a small distance away and upon investigation found some men fishing. He told them that the fish were his and that they had no right to let the water out of the pond that served the yard until he had done with using it. He requested that they stop the water flow and repair the bay, at which **William Tyler** was very abusive and told him to do it himself. As he went back he put the penstock into its place to secure the water. Then after feeding his cattle, he fetched a padlock from the barn in order to lock the penstock down.

As he approached, the two young men he had seen fishing at the upper pond, ran to the penstock, pulled it out and carried it away. He chased after them and suddenly one of them stopped short and in consequence he ran into him and knocked him over into some gorse bushes. The man got up, and said *"Damn me, what did you knock me into the furze for"* and he struck Markbee with a violent blow which knocked him down and cut both sides of his face. The person who knocked him down, now known to be **John Tyler**, knelt on his stomach and held him by the collar until he had almost choked on the blood that had run into his mouth and swore that he should not get up. Several times, John Tyler called out *"Mr Tyler, Mr Tyler"*, then William Tyler, being at the upper pond, about 13 Rod (about 70 yards) away, lading water said *"Let him get up"*.

John Tyler tried to get off William Markbee, but the padlock, which Markbee had in his hands, hooked onto Tyler's frock (coat). Tyler said *"Let go of my frock"*, but before Markbee could disentangle the padlock, Tyler turned and gave him another violent punch in the stomach. Thus winded, Markbee lay on the ground for quite a while. When he did get up, he saw William Tyler standing there with his fists raised saying *"Damn me, if you strike the lad I'm your man"*. In the fall, Markbee had dropped the key to the padlock. He was looking around for it when Tyler said *"What are you looking for? There's the key"*, and he picked it up and threw it into the pond. He then grabbed the padlock, in Markbee's hand and after a struggle, wrenched it free and threw that into the pond also.

Markbee then said that he hoped that William Tyler was satisfied and he went off to fetch a neighbour, **Mr Garrard,** or some of his family, to come to identify the persons who had attacked him. Mr Garrard happened to be at home and asked Mr Markbee what had happened since he was in such a bloody state. Mr Garrard agreed to accompany him and found the person in the ground gate hole. He identified him as John Tyler, son of William Tyler. Tyler then carried the fish down to the lower pond and Garrard and Markbee followed. William Tyler counted 62 fish into the pond. Markbee then insisted that they should secure the ponds and mend the bay. The Tylers said that they had orders for what they did and they then went away cursing Markbee and Garrard for identifying them.

Editorial comment; there was another case of assault on William Markbee by James Packham on the highway in 1798, about which attempts were made to bring about a settlement before it came up at the next Quarter Sessions.(HM MSS Cat. No. 288.136 and 137). This suggests that on this occasion Markbee may have given some provocation to his attacker.

Horsham Museum MSS Cat. No. 360, *extracted by* **John Hurd**

The King againt James Stenning of Wisborough Green labourer, for assault

Easter Sessions 1792

Pleaded not guilty; *Endorsed:* convicted, sentenced 6 months imprisonment in solitude in Petworth House of Correction. *Endorsed with a note:* bad as his character in other respects - son was with James Edwards.

Case for the prosecution

On 20th January 1792 **John Older**[3] spent the evening in a friendly game of cards at **Mr Henry Smart's** at Pallands Farm in Wisborough Green, about 2 miles from home.[4] He stayed until about 3 am; he was perfectly sober and set off home; there was no moon but it was a very light morning. He stopped to ease himself and heard footsteps behind him; thinking it was **Abraham Cooper**, one of the company at Smart's he greeted him but there was no reply. He discovered it was not Cooper but recognised **James Stenning** and seeing that he was striking across a field offered to accompany him because they lived near each other. Stenning seemed to want to avoid him so Older said, *"What signifies your shying from me, I don't want to know what you have got in your sack - you have got none of my property, Master Stenning."* Stenning threw down the sack (which seemed to be about two bushels of corn) and struck Older with his staff which had a piece of iron shaped like a farmer's billhook. Older fell down, losing his hat (which was found the following day by Abraham Cooper as he returned from Smart's). Older recovered and followed Stenning but when he got about 2 rods from him Stenning again threw down the sack and threatened him with his stick. Older said, *"You good for nothing old dog - I bleed so much I cannot stop with you now but I know you very well and I'll let you know if these be any Law for you another day."*

Two men, W.H. Pyne, *(Etchings of Rustic Figures)*

Older went home bleeding and sought the assistance of **Isaac Morris** a surgeon who lived next door. At about 8 am the same morning Older went to Stenning's house with Henry Smart's son and found him in bed. Stenning said that he had been in bed since 6 or 7 the preceding evening. On 21st January James Stenning was arrested and 16th March **Mr. Evans**, secretary of the Wisborough Green Prosecuting Society, wrote to **Mr Medwin** appointing him as prosecutor.[5] On 16th April Stenning appeared at Midhurst Quarter Sessions. He was found guilty. In court **Christopher Stenning** swore that he went to his father's house in Wisborough Green at about 3.30pm previous to the morning when James Older was assaulted. He found his father fully dressed sitting on the side of his bed in a very bad state of health; he undressed and went to bed and Christopher was with him almost continuously until about 8 the next morning.

---

[3]   Sussex Record Society, Vol. 82, *West Sussex Land Tax 1785,* Wisbrough Green, pp. 242-7. John Older lived at the *Three Crowns* in Wisborough Green, owned by Henry Ede, in 1785.
[4]   As above. Henry Smart is said in the Land Tax records to live at Papelands Farm.
[5]   Probably the Rev. Morgan Evans, curate of Wisbrough Green and Kirdford, who had previously sought Medwin's assistance in another case (see Chapter 12, case 327)

Memorandum 21st April 1792 - The King vs Christopher Stenning for perjury

On 21st April Mr. Evans, Mr Wells and Mr Older went to the *Kings Head* at Kirdford; **Mrs Boxall** said that **Christopher Stenning** came in about dusk on the Friday evening *(in January)* and said that Mr Older's head was cut; he bought a pint of rum and said that his wife had sent for the midwife. Mrs Boxall was sure about the night in question because she asked Stenning whether his sisters would be attending a dance at her house that evening as one of the sisters was with Christopher Stenning's wife - both did attend the dance. **Mr Boxall** recollected seeing Christopher Stenning at the *King's Head*. **Mrs Randall** the midwife confirmed that she had attended **Mrs Stenning** at Stroud Green - she confirmed that Christopher Stenning had been to Mrs Boxall for rum - also that she had seen him at his home at different intervals all that night.

6 Aug. 1792 - Receipt from **William Cooper** of the *Green Dragon* (Bishopric):

Expenses for Witnesses

Beer	5s
Spirits	1s. 6d
Dinners	13. 6d
Gin & Water	2s. 9d
Corn & hay	3s. 3d
(Total)	£1.6s

Editorial comment; This receipt is included as it shows the lengths to which Thomas Charles Medwin went to get the witnesses to appear at the Assizes, and also because it shows him giving business to his former servant, William Cooper, now innkeeeper of the Green Dragon *(see Appendix).*

An Inn Kitchen, c. 1800, *Thomas Rowlandson*

Horsham Museum MSS Cat. No. 364, *extracted by* **Norman Hewell.**

The King vs Frances Cooper for Assault on Sarah Marsh at Horsham

Midsummer Sessions 1794

The case for the defence

The parents of the prosecutor who is about twelve years old and the parents of the defendant who is about thirteen years old, inhabit tenements adjoining each other, situated in East Street, Horsham. Several disputes and quarrels between the two mothers, each upholding and protecting their families of numerous children against the other, has caused ill feeling between these neighbours. There are eight children in each family and it is no wonder that amongst so many of almost equal age, repeated little fights have taken place. On 5th July 1793, the mother of **Sarah Marsh** went out and left orders that Sarah was to make sure that her little brother, who was very small, went to school in his mother's absence. The boy refused to go, so Sarah pushed him down, grabbed his hair and began to beat his head on the ground. William Harding, the Constable, was up a ladder painting a house which belonged to him, opposite to the happening, and there were several other onlookers. **Frances Cooper** was there, seeing to her brothers and sisters, because her mother was in the garden attending to her washing. The adults present, requested that Frances go to the rescue of the little boy, before his sister did him some damage. Accordingly, Frances went and endeavoured to take the little boy away from his sister, whereupon Sarah tore her cap from her head and threw stones at her. This so annoyed Frances that she took a small stick which was lying in the street and a scuffle ensued, the stick frequently changing hands. This fight continued until a neighbour separated them.

It is a little unusual for a case like this to come to court, but the parents of Sarah Marsh, due to the ill feelings between them and their neighbours, and stimulated by meddling, officious people, thought it proper to prefer an indictment. So now, the quarrel of two children is to be seriously discussed in a court of justice and to be tried by the oaths of a jury and as **Mr Ellis**, who is now concerned in this prosecution, has thought it proper to make a point of collecting witnesses to prove the assault and to magnify, as much as possible, the violence of it, it has become necessary to contact persons who saw the whole of the incident and get them to speak on behalf of the defendant, to protect her from punishment.

It will be pretended that Sarah was violently bruised by Frances and that several of her finger nails were torn off, but the fact is that she hurt her fingers with a stone on the previous day and her struggle for the stick caused the nail to be torn and bleed. That same evening, after the fight, Sarah's father, upon returning from work and hearing about the quarrel, was very angry and beat her for it. If Sarah is called as a witness, please cross-examine her as to the hurt on her finger and on her father's beating on that same evening. Please also cross-examine **Sarah Rowland** and **Elizabeth Laker** whether she did not first beat her little brother in the manner described and afterwards tear off the defendant's cap and throw stones at her when she endeavoured to rescue the little boy.

As witnesses for the defence we can call upon **Mrs Elizabeth Bourne** who lived opposite, **Mrs Sarah Mills** who lived next door and **Mr William Harding** who was painting a house opposite and who is a Constable. All of them saw what happened.

Editorial comment. The Marshes were probably descendants of Abel Marsh, gardener, who lived in East Street and had a property there. In her diary for 1760, Sarah Hurst records on 15 June; "Walk up to Abel Marsh, a gardener's, & see a Sun Dial made with greens, a great curiosity". The Rowlands were bricklayers and stone-masons, and later had a builders' yard just to the west of the Sussex County Gaol in East Street.

The King (on the prosecution of Mr William Cooper) vs Dendy Napper for assault

Epiphany Sessions at Chichester 1805

Indictment for assault at Warnham on 2nd April 1804 - preferred at the last Midhurst Sessions which the defendant (**Dendy Napper**) "traversed" *(sic)*.   *(This means that he formally contradicted or denied the charge)*.

The case for the prosecution

The prosecutor, **William Cooper,** is an innkeeper at Horsham and has a farm at Warnham.   Dendy Napper the defendant is also a farmer at Warnham. Napper had a former quarrel with William Cooper when he instigated and supported **Benjamin Boorer** to dispute a Will made in Cooper's favour regarding some land in Warnham. *(Benjamim Boorer's case - a civil action - against William Cooper had just been heard at the Spring Quarter Sessions in Horsham at the time of the assault.   Details of the Benjamin Boorer case are in the Appendix).*

Edward James, formerly of Horsham, brazier, but who now keeps the *White Horse Inn* at Steyning, accompanied William Cooper to a farm he occupied in Warnham on Easter Monday 2nd April 1804 to enquire of the bailiff whether it would be advantageous to him to retain a Parish boy and girl at the Parish Vestry Meeting at Warnham that evening.   On Cooper's return from the farm he found that the meeting had adjourned to one of the public houses at Warnham and, not knowing which, *The Bell* or *The Marquis of Granby,* he called first at the *Marquis of Granby* to enquire.   On going into the kitchen, Mr Cooper called for a pint of beer and he and James sat down on a form in the middle of the kitchen.   Dendy Napper was sitting on a chair in the chimney corner drinking - the moment he saw Cooper he cried out *"Do tell how was it you and your little Medwin did bring your cause to the Assizes!"*   Cooper replied *"Twas no fault of mine!"* and desired him not to concern himself with other peoples' affairs.   Napper became so abusive that **Mr Agate** and **Mr Redford** removed themselves to another room.   Cooper followed with James and went to the parlour where they found Agate, Redford and a soldier, the servant of **Captain Money**.

Redford spoke to Cooper about the cause and asked why it had not been brought to trial and Cooper gave the same answer he gave to Napper.   Captain Money's servant vindicated Redford and added that neither Cooper nor James had any business in the room.   Cooper replied that he had more business being there than Money's servant had, to which he replied that Cooper was a liar - Cooper retorted, *"If you call me a liar again I'll knock you out of your chair!"*   Money's servant struck Cooper so violently on the head that he fell from his seat.   Cooper then said *"I sha'n't take this, let me get up and I'll fight it out fairly".*   They began fighting and both fell together, Cooper being uppermost.   The noise brought Napper into the room and whilst Cooper was attempting to rise, Napper caught him by the coat and waistcoat near his neck and pushed him with great violence over a chair in the corner of the room.   James advised Cooper to stop, to which Cooper said, *"I will and I've done".*   Having sat down, Cooper said to Napper *"You have no business to strike me".*   To this Napper said *"I have not yet - but I will now!"* and immediately struck him violently in the face until blood came from Cooper's nose and mouth and gave him two black eyes; he continued his blows until he became weary.   Napper's conduct during the whole of the business was spiteful and brutal in the extreme and James was really apprehensive that some serious injury would be done.

At about 4 pm Cooper and James quitted the house and went to *The Bell* where the Parish Officers were met. Having settled with them they left for Horsham; Napper, however, closely followed them.   As Cooper and James left *The Bell,* Cooper took out a pistol from his pocket, saying, *"It is lucky it did not go off!"*   This was the first time James observed him to have any pistol and is confident that Cooper did not take it from his pocket at any time before this.   On his return home Cooper told James that he had begun travelling with pistols since recent robberies involving persons of the name of Knight and Ansell in the neighbourhood of Horsham. *(On 2nd January 1803, **Thomas Ansell,** jun. was returning from Horsham market with £100 in his pocket when he was stopped near the Dog and Bacon on Horsham Common by a footpad who demanded the money.   He successfully resisted the attack as he was quite young and strong.   This is the same Thomas*

Ansell who was involved in a case of attempted rape in 1783 - see case 319, Chapter 9. But on the very same evening **Mr. Knight**, *a farmer of Bourne Hill, was knocked down and robbed of three £1 notes and a 7s. gold piece).*[6]

On the following day James saw Cooper with a cut under his eye and both eyes very black; his face & nose were very black and swollen and covered in bruises. Cooper had sent for a surgeon who deemed it necessary to bleed him. The black eyes and other bruises on Cooper's face were not given by Money's servant. Cooper believed that, had not Napper interfered, he would have beaten him. All the blows to his face were given him by Napper. The defence may attempt to suggest that Napper only interfered as second to Captain Money's servant and that the whole was a drunken affray in a public house and Parish Meeting: **Mr Edward James** will testify that Cooper was sober at the time.

Napper is a man of considerable property but very much given to drunkenness and quarrels. It is hoped that the Court will inflict such punishment on him as will operate as an example to others and deter him from committing such outrages in future.

Editorial comment: Dendy Napper was a wealthy farmer who owned the Manor of Slaughterford and Powers, and acted as overseer of the poor in Warnham. In the 1806 Land Tax for Warnham, he was rated at £142, on a par with Sir Bysshe Shelley, who owned the Great Tithes (£80) plus Baylings Farm and other properties with a total rental of £61. The next highest rated farmer was John Agate, who had properties worth £60 and £30. So the final comment seems quite justified.

Two men outside a public house, Bowes and Carver

---

[6]   William Albery, *Millennium*, p. 247.

The Queen vs Mary Hall junior, for attacking her Mother with a knife

Lent Assizes – 17th March 1845

Indictment for *"having on 4th October last unlawfully and maliciously stabbed, cut and wounded Mary Hall senior (the prisoner's Mother) with intent to maim, disfigure or disable or to do some other grievous bodily harm"*.

The following evidence will be given as proof by the prosecutor;

Mary Hall senior, the prisoner's Mother. She will testify that on 8th August last, the prisoner had an illegitimate child, which died within one week of birth, that she had a good confinement and was tolerably well until after the child's death. That she then had milk fever and one of her breasts broke and her mind was a good deal affected at times and she complained of pain at the back part of her head. That she came downstairs about a fortnight after her confinement and her headache continued and her breast was very bad. She was attended by **Mr Bourne**, a surgeon at Horsham, and a witness for the prisoner during her confinement and subsequently. Mr Bourne gave the witness *(Mrs. Hall)* a caution that she ought to be very careful about her daughter as she appeared not to know what she was doing at times and in consequence of this caution, the back doors were kept locked since there is a deep well in the yard, which though covered, is close to the doors.

About a week after she came downstairs, on 25th August, a Sunday when the witness was in the front shop, fishmonger and fruiterer, run by her and her husband, she had left the prisoner in the kitchen, apparently asleep by the fire. The prisoner contrived to open one of the doors and threw herself into the well. Some alarm was given by a neighbour, about the well, and the witness went to look for the prisoner; the witness found that the back door was open and on entering the yard found that the lid was on the well. She searched the yard, but was alarmed by a noise like a groan, apparently coming from the well. She lifted the lid and saw the prisoner rising to the surface of the water, 33 to 34 feet below. The witness called for help and several of her neighbours came to her assistance. She unwound the chain and rope from the well curb and let them down into the well. The prisoner took hold of the chain and was pulled out by two neighbours (Penfold and his brother). The prisoner was almost unconscious and was taken upstairs and put to bed. She opened her eyes whilst they were undressing her and said *"Oh mother, don't cry"*. **Mr Thomas**, another surgeon at Horsham, and his assistant had arrived in the mean time and Mr Thomas advised the witness to leave the room, which she did.

The witness or her daughter Betsy had occasionally slept with the prisoner from the time of the child's death and she continued to do so until the occurrence which is the subject of the present investigation. The witness went to see the prisoner as soon as she was to some degree recovered, but she seemed very bad and did not speak to the witness or anyone else at that time. She later said that she did not know how she had got into the well, she became better in a few days and went about her household and other work as usual, but she complained frequently about her head. She was at times very dejected and low spirited. On the 4th October, the witness had been out to a neighbour **Mr Collett** to get change for half a crown and on her return, the prisoner said *"Where have you been so long, gossiping about me?"*. The witness said *"Your name has not been mentioned"*. The prisoner had the bellows in her hand and had been blowing the fire to make the kettle boil in readiness for tea. The prisoner threw the bellows at the witness and they fell on her feet. The witness said *"Mary, what do you mean by that?"*. She stopped to pick up the bellows and while she was bending down, she felt something cut her neck. She put her hand to her neck and it was covered with blood. The prisoner had something in her hand, which she placed on the table, and although the witness did not see what it was, she supposed it was a knife since there were two or three on the table. The witness pulled off her apron, bound it round her neck and went upstairs. The prisoner followed her and upon entering the room, said *"Oh mother, what have I done?"*; and her mother replied *"Don't say anything and nobody will know about it"*. The prisoner took off her apron and bound it about her mother's neck. Witness went back downstairs and some time later the prisoner followed.

When her son Henry came home and saw his mother's neck, he asked what had happened and she told him that Mary had done it. He went out to call for assistance and Jeremiah Collett, Mr. Penfold, Mrs Lovekin and John Rapson came and later, Mr Lovegrove arrived. He is another surgeon at Horsham and he dressed the neck and stayed with the witness until she had recovered.

Jeremiah Collett, **Mrs Lovekin** and **Penfold** will testify that they answered **Henry Hall's** call for help and will say how they found Mrs Hall and of the circumstances implicating or tending to implicate the prisoner. **Mr Joseph Lovegrove** will testify to the nature of the injury inflicted upon Mrs Hall and that in his opinion, the wound found in her neck was caused by some cutting instrument. **John Rapson**, sergeant of a recruiting party stationed at Horsham, will testify that he also entered the house of Mrs Hall and her husband and he went upstairs and in one of the bedrooms he found the prisoner standing alone, she had blood on her dress and there was blood on the floor near where she stood. She said that someone was making a great noise, but he told her that he could not hear any noise. She again said that someone was making a great noise and that it was going through her head. Her brother came to the foot of the stairs and she asked who it was. Rapson said it was her brother but she did not believe him. She then came downstairs with him and he took her into a room away from her mother and the others. He says that she did not know what she was about and she was cold and shaking.

Evidence on behalf of the prisoner

Mr Thomas Bourne – Surgeon - will testify that he attended the prisoner in her confinement, that she was delivered of a child which lived about six days, that one of her breast was broken and she was in a feverish, excited state after her confinement and that she was not a person of strong intellect. That in consequence of a conversation with the prisoner's mother, and the situation of the well in the yard near to the house, that the back doors be kept locked. That he had heard of the prisoner's act of attempted suicide, a fortnight after the confinement and the evidence given during this trial regarding the present charge and will declare his belief that at the time of these two incidents the prisoner was not in her right mind.

Mr Mance – the keeper of the prison at Petworth - will, as the prisoner's solicitor is instructed, testify that the prisoner's conduct has been obedient and exemplary during the five months of her detention.

Mrs M. A. Thorns - a certificate is attached from the prisoner's former mistress, Mrs M. A. Thorns, that the prisoner, whilst in her employ from 15th June 1842 to 20th April 1843, conducted herself in an orderly manner, and as Mrs Thorns is prevented by illness from attending the trial it may perhaps be used at least in mitigation of punishment, should a verdict of guilty be returned.

Observations for the prisoner

The prisoner's solicitor was only instructed on Saturday and can therefore do little more than state the proofs as they will be cited on the trial. The committing magistrate, **Mr Hurst**, took a lenient and merciful view of the evidence, and committed the prisoner for trial for the minor offence only, of wounding, with intent to do some grievous bodily harm and it is believed that the indictment against the prisoner will be framed with the same view. It is moreover in the prisoner's favour that no prosecution has been ordered, especially that the prisoner's father was not called upon to enter into a recognizance, either to prosecute or for the appearance of his wife to give evidence.

The mother therefore appears upon a subpoena, which does not extend to call upon her to attend and give evidence before a grand jury, to attend the assizes and testify the truth and give evidence against the prisoner upon the trial. With which act and the further act of binding over the other witnesses for the prosecution in the usual manner to appear and give evidence before the grand jury and afterwards upon the prisoner's trial.

Mr Stedman, the magistrates' clerk, has ended his official duty on the present occasion – the conduct of the proceedings will thus rest with the clerk of the Assize, subject to the Lord Chief Justice's direction, and who it is presumed will place the sworn evidence in the hands of one of the learned counsel to examine the witnesses and carry on the prosecution upon the prisoner's trial.

The case for the defence

It will be seen that the case is of a bad complexion. There is no proof, however, of malice existing, on the contrary, the fact of the prisoner sleeping with her mother must have led to a reciprocal feeling of kindness between them and it is hoped that under the circumstances to be detailed in the mother's evidence, malice will not be presumed, but the court and the jury may be induced, as far as they can, to look with mercy and consideration upon the unfortunate prisoner's conduct. The defence, so far as it depends upon the state of mind of the prisoner, is somewhat dangerous, for if it should lead to a verdict of acquittal on the grounds of temporary insanity it may cause the prisoner's perpetual imprisonment. It can hardly however be omitted with safety and it is submitted that it may be brought forward in aid of the first suggested line of defence, and may help to show the absence of malice.

Editorial comment: The 1840 Tithe Map and Schedule *for the town centre (published by Horsham Museum Society in 1998) enable us to find out exactly where this incident took place. The list of neighbours given in the account of the suicide attempt acts as confirmation.* Richard Hall, *fishmonger, lived in a house on the south-west corner of the Carfax island - no. 402 on the schedule (more or less where the* Sussex Camera Centre *is today).* The Penfolds *lived next door at no. 401, and* Jeremish Collett *is known to have been a baker living in the alley across the road - still known as* Collett's Alley *(though he does not appear in the Tithe Map schedule, which was drawn up five years earlier).*

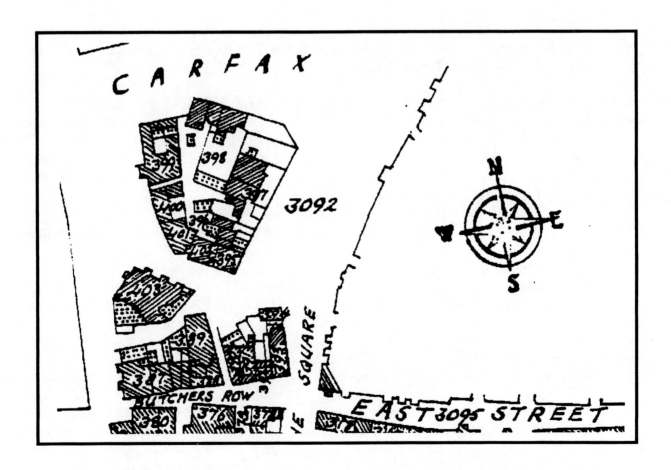

Map of the Carfax - redrawn from the Horsham Tithe Map by Alan Siney

ℰ Chapter Two - Burglary ℛ

Horsham Museum MSS Cat. No. 348 *by John Hurd*

The King (on the prosecution of Mr John Laker vs William Stenning for Burglary

Sussex: Summer Assizes at Lewes 31ˢᵗ July 1789

The case for the prosecution

Between 5 and 6 am on 9ᵗʰ May 1789 **William Laker,** son of **John Laker** tailor & salesman of Billingshurst, informed his father that the shop had been broken open and robbed. A pane of glass was broken and the window was wide open. Among the stolen items were:

- a man's blue coat
- a man's drab cloth coat
- a <u>Marseilles white linen waistcoat</u>
- sundry other coats and waistcoats partly made up
- several garments not made up
- one pound of silk and twist
- one pound of thread and two pairs of scissors
- remnants of fustian etc

The shop had been broken into four times in 7 years; the last time about 4 years previously **James Stenning** of Wisborough Green (father of the prisoner, **William Stenning**) was seen on the evening of the robbery lurking in the garden of **James Knight.**

The prisoner William Stenning, with his brothers John & James and their father had all been repeatedly indicted and tried for various felonies. At the Epiphany Sessions 1785 John Stenning was convicted and received sentence of Transportation - but William *"had the good luck to escape the hands of Justice".* The father and sons had no visible means of obtaining a livelihood but for many years supported themselves by thieving, pilfering and committing depradations upon the property of those unfortunate enough to reside in their neighbourhood, *"to whom they are a terror"*

John Laker suspected William Stenning but waited until Friday 3ʳᵈ July to obtain a Warrant from **William Smith** of Stopham to search the house of William Stenning. On Saturday 4ᵗʰ July John Laker, his son William, the Constable and three other assistants searched the house (the prisoner was not at home). In the entrance room, in a dry tub amongst some leather straps and lumber, they found the Marseilles waistcoat, which had a private mark of the sale price in ink on the lining. The Warrant permitted a search of the houses of known associates. **Edwards** of Sweetwater Pond near Whitely in Surrey was an associate. Armed with a brace of pistols John Laker went in pursuit of Stenning and on enquiry traced him as far as Roundstreet Common about two miles from his house, but did not find him. On the evening of Saturday 11ᵗʰ John Laker, with son William and four assistants went to Stenning's house but he was not there.

William Stenning had been bound over to answer a charge of fowl stealing at the last Horsham Sessions. **William Scardefield** had been employed to watch Stenning and at about 5-6 am on 14ᵗʰ he reported that Stenning was at the Crown Inn at Horsham. John Laker got **Sharp** the Constable and they found William Stenning in bed with his uncle **Richardson** who stood as bail for his appearance at the Sessions. They took Stenning into custody and took him before magistrate **Mr Aldridge** who committed the prisoner to Horsham Gaol.

(There follow details of the shop/premises - with legal precedents to prove that the charge was burglary- which differs from theft in that it involves breaking and entering a house)

Proofs for the Prosecutor:

George Stemp. James Stenning the father of William came to his workplace near Arundel on the --- day of July & desired him to swear that his son William bought a waistcoat from him at Green Fair.

Charles Best. William Stenning and a woman with whom he cohabited at his house in Steyning from --- to --- brought with them divers articles of clothing and amongst then was a blue cloth coat; a drab cloth coat; printed cotton waistcoat of the pattern and buttons which will be produced and had been made up at Steyning

Mr John Laker. Among the stolen goods was a printed cotton waistcoat and 7/8 printed cotton the same as that which the prisoner had made up - also be will produce a button to match those on the blue coat.

Editorial comment: This is another instance of one of the Stenning family being in trouble - see also Chapters One and Twelve.

Four studies of men in various styles of dress, W.H. Pyne *(Etchings of Rustic Figures)*

Two men in the pillory

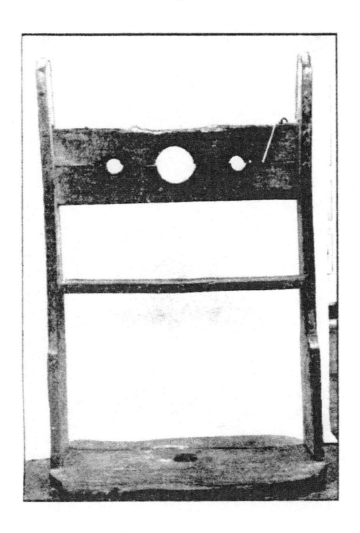

The pillory at Rye (old photograph from William Albery's *Millennium*)

❧ Chapter Three - Conspiracy in aiding the escape of French prisoners ❦

Horsham Museum MSS Cat. No. 435, *transcribed by Norman Hewell*

Petition from John Hughes, gaoled for conspiracy in aiding French Prisoners to escape.

Lewes Assizes - 1ˢᵗ August 1812

John Hughes petitioning from Horsham Gaol, where he had been sent for two years by the Right Honourable Edward Lord Ellenborough, sitting at Lewes on 1ˢᵗ August 1812, having been convicted together with **James Robinson** of a conspiracy in aiding the escape of **Gene Phillipson** and **Louis Garnier**, French prisoners from Shropshire to Rye and thence to France.   He complains that within the first month in gaol, he was taken and put into a pillory near Rye, within view of the French coast, for an hour. He felt this to be a most ignominious punishment in addition to his time in Horsham Gaol.

He also complains that a letter which he wrote to James Robinson stating that *"Alls Well"* did not refer to the escape of these prisoners, but to some watches and other contraband goods which he had sold for Robinson, and that a witness, **Thomas Clark**, together with five other witnesses who attended the trial, were not called by his counsel. His only contact with Robinson was with regard to contraband goods for which he had acted as agent, when Robinson had occasionally stayed at the *Red Lyon Inn* in Rye, which Hughes ran, and that he has nothing to do with the transaction for which he had been put in such deep disgrace and infamy.

At the end of June, beginning of July 1812 at about ten o'clock at night, on a Thursday, a carriage and pair came to the *Red Lyon Inn* at Rye. There were only a post boy and a servant with the carriage and the servant told John Hughes that James Robinson was coming and the carriage then went into the yard. Half an hour later, Robinson arrived on his own and there was no indication that anyone had been in the carriage or elsewhere with him. Robinson said that he would not stop that night and that the carriage would be sent away in the morning. He was gone within half an hour, and when Hughes got up in the morning, the carriage was gone. He heard no more about Robinson till the following Saturday when a police officer came from London and said that the carriage had been traced to the *Red Lyon Inn* at Rye and that it had contained two French officers. Hughes said that only a post boy and a servant had come with the carriage.

On the following Monday, Robinson was arrested in Shropshire and sent a letter to Hughes asking him to send to the *New Inn*, in the town where he was arrested, a horse and gig. Hughes sent word that he had none to send and that Robinson had been to the *Red Lyon* on several occasions but that only once did he have anyone with him and that was on a Saturday when they came on the London coach and stayed for one night. The visitor left at about 11 o'clock the next morning, Hughes did not see him, but Robinson said that he had gone to Tunbridge Wells and that his name was Smith and that he was a countryman of his.

He stated that the above was fully supported by James Robinson and confirmed by Thomas Clark and there were character references from people who knew him at the *Red Lyon* at Rye and also from his master's accountant at Rye and from the Postmaster who had been at Rye for fourteen years.

Editorial comment; this case reminds us that Britain had been at war with France for nearly twenty years, since 1793, and that there had been good reason for Sussex to fear an invasion by Napoleon's troops in 1804. It can be appreciated that any suspicion of aiding French prisoners to escape would be severely punished; smuggling too was not regarded with as much tolerance as it had been formerly, since it meant dealing with the enemy.

Springfield Place in Horsham, from the painting by Sydney Arrobus

Shopping in the market , W.H. Pyne *(Etchings of Rustic Figures)*

Horsham Museum MSS Cat. No. 422, *extracted by* **Sheila Stevens**

The King (on the prosecution of John Morris Esquire) against Ann Golding, for felony

Petworth Michaelmas Sessions 1806

(Editorial comments on the document - Mr Doyly   2gns.   Acquitted. Medwin,   Horsham)

The prisoner was committed to Petworth about a month ago and will be indicted at the present sessions for receiving money from the prosecutor (her master) as his housekeeper, and fraudulently embezzling part thereof by signing the name **C. Dendy** to bills for butter and other small family articles whereby she obtained from her master the amount of such bills and secreted and did not pay the same over to the said C. Dendy.

The case for the prosecution

This prosecution is founded on an Act of Parliament passed the 12th July 1799 (39th Geo 3rd cap 85) entitled *"An Act to protect masters against embezzlements by their clerks or servants"* whereby after reciting that

> *"whereas Bankers Merchants and others are, in the course of their dealings and transactions frequently obliged to entrust their servants, clerks and persons employed by them in the like capacity with receiving paying negotiating exchanging or transferring money goods bonds bills notes bankers drafts and other valuable effects and securities and whereas doubts have been entertained whether the embezzling of the same by such servants clerks and others so employed by their masters amounts to felony by the law of England and it is expedient that such offenders should be punished in the same manner in both parts of the United Kingdom. It is enacted that if any servant or clerk or any person employed for the purpose in the capacity of a servant or clerk to any person or persons whomsoever or to any body corporate or politick shall by virtue of such employment receive or take into his possession any money goods bond bill note bankers draft or other valuable security or effects for or in the name or on the account of his master or masters ... and every such offender his adviser procurer aider or abettor being thereof lawfully convicted or attainted shall be liable to be transported to such parts beyond the seas as His Majesty by and with the advice of his Privy Council shall appoint for any term not exceeding fourteen years in the discretion of the court before whom such offender shall be convicted or adjudged."*

The frequent frauds and embezzlements by servants of their master's property (which used to be considered as mere Breaches of Trust and could only be sued for at Common Law) called for the interference of the Legislature in making the above statute, declaring the offence punishable as a felony.

The prosecutor, **John Morris Esq.,** in the Spring of 1805, took a mansion house called Springfield Place, with the contiguous lawn and meadows, situate at Horsham in Sussex, which had then lately been occupied by **Mrs Osbaldeston**, and came to reside there with his family in or about the month of June in that year. Previous to Mr Morris coming to take up his residence at Horsham he had hired the prisoner, **Ann Golding**, as his housekeeper and from the character he had received of her did not entertain any doubt of her honesty. Mr Morris has habits of great correctness in the regulation of his household establishment making it, at that time, a rule to settle his Butcher's, Baker's and other bills for small articles used in his family weekly . On his arrival at Horsham he adopted this mode with the prisoner who accompanied him thither in the said capacity of housekeeper. Among other tradespeople with whom Mr Morris dealt at Horsham were persons of the name of **Thomas** and **Cassandra Dendy,** Thomas Dendy, the husband, carrying on the business of a corn chandler and Cassandra, his wife, dealing in butter, vinegar, salt and other articles usually sold in chandler's shops.

The prisoner, in consequence of her master's directions, delivered in weekly bills, sometimes in the name of T. Dendy and at other times in that of C. Dendy, receipted at the bottom by **Sarah Lampard** (who assisted in the shop).   Occasionally the bills were in her own name but more frequently in the name of C. Dendy, and thereupon Mr Morris paid her the amount of such bills and took them as vouchers. This practice regularly continued through the whole of the summer and up to the 18ᵗʰ November 1805 when Mr Morris and his family left the County to reside during the winter in London.

At this period, although the prosecutor had thus regularly settled with the prisoner her weekly accounts and paid her the amount thereof as before stated, it seems that she then stood indebted to T. and C. Dendy in the sum of £11. 13s. 10d., which she had received of Mr Morris but not paid over.   Just before the family went to London, the prisoner called on Mrs Dendy and told her that as her master and herself had not settled accounts she hoped if it would make no difference if she did not then pay her the whole amount of her bills, then paying her £5 on account thereof and promising to pay the residue in a short time after her arrival in town, to a person in Southwark with whom Mrs Dendy dealt for oranges. But not hearing of any payment and a considerable time having elapsed, Mrs Dendy enquired of her orange merchant whether any person had paid him money on her account, who, having answered in the negative, T. Dendy, her husband wrote to the prisoner reminding her of the neglect of her promise, whereupon she then sent Mrs Dendy a one pound note and excused her want of punctuality by stating (what was an absolute falsehood) that the family had been all ill and herself so much confined on that account that she could not get time to go into Southwark to pay the money, but would shortly send it by the Horsham Carrier. This promise however, she did not perform with more punctuality than the former, and thus matters rested till the family returned to Horsham in the summer of 1806, when fresh dealings took place with T. and C. Dendy and Mr Morris, instead of paying his bills weekly, then adopted the plan of paying them monthly, as being attended with less trouble to himself. The amount of such monthly bills exceeding 40s., regular stamps were given by the before named Sarah Lampard for, or in the name of T. Dendy or his wife, and Mr Morris had not the slightest suspicion that any sum whatever was demandable of him by the said T. and C. Dendy.

Repeated applications to the prisoner were made by Thomas and Cassandra Dendy for payment of the former account. Without being able to obtain the same, she, many times excusing herself by saying that her master and herself had outstanding accounts on which much money was due to her, and particularly desiring that no application might be made to Mr Morris (who might take offence thereat), they refrained from informing him of the transaction. But on or about the 11ᵗʰ August last, Mrs Dendy thought proper to relate the circumstance to Mr Morris's gardener, who then mentioned the same to his master and then he, on reference to the weekly bills delivered by the prisoner, and application to Mrs Dendy, discover'd that from the 12ᵗʰ of August to the 18ᵗʰ of November 1805 they were all written and receipted at bottom C. Dendy, not by her, her husband or the said Sarah Lampard (who kept the accounts), but in the handwriting of the prisoner, and that £5 still remained due for goods sold during that period for which Mr Morris, as before stated, had paid the prisoner, and that she had embezzled the money and applied it to her own use.

This discovery naturally induced Mr Morris, on his return to Town, to make the necessary enquiries amongst his tradesmen in order to learn whether the prisoner had been guilty of similar practices during the time his family resided there, when he discovered that she had done so to a considerable extent, which determined him on returning to Horsham to prosecute the prisoner for the embezzlement under the statute hereinbefore stated, conceiving himself bound so to do for the sake of public justice and to deter servants entrusted with their masters' property from such nefarious conduct.

Proofs for the prosecutor

To prove the payment by the prosecutor to the prisoner of   )   **John Morris Esqʳ** (who will
the amount of the several bills purporting to be the bills of   )   produce the said bills with
T. & C. Dendy from the 12ᵗʰ August to the 18ᵗʰ November   )   receipts at the foot fabricated
1805 (inclusive) the subsequent demand of payment of part   )   by and in the handwriting of
of such bills from him by said Thoˢ & Cassandra Dendy   )   the prisoner.)
and the other circumstances herein before stated.   Call   )

To prove that the bills from 12th Aug[st] to 18th Nov[r] 1805 are not of)
the handwriting of S. Lampard (who kept her accounts) or of)
T. Dendy (her husband) The circumstances that passed between)
herself and the prisoner respecting the payment of the balance of) **Cassandra Dendy**
the bills delivered to the prisoner within the period before mentioned)
and that £5 still remains due thereon from the prosecutor.   Call)

Note on the cover page:

The prisoner was acquitted on an indictment proffered for larceny in stealing 1 Horsham Bank Note of £5, 5 Horsham Bank Notes of £1 each and £2 of monies numbered - for although Mr Morris proved the payment to the prisoner of a one pound Horsham Bank Note on the 18 November 1805, she might have paid that away in discharge of bills and the note could not be identified. The Council thought the offence did not come within the statute 39 George III, that being meant to cover money paid by a third person or persons for or on account of the master, and not paid or advanced by the master to the servant to discharge bills really due, but which the servant neglected to do. This money being due when paid to the servant for the above debt, could not either be hold as obtaining it under false pretences, and thus the prisoner escaped punishment.

Editorial comment.   Nothing else is known of John Morris, who is one of many tenants who rented Springfield Park from the Blunt family, after the death of Samuel Blunt (its builder) in 1800.   But the Dendys were a well-known family in the Horsham district, with many branches.   Thomas Dendy, the corn-chandler, was quite possibly the Thomas who was born in 1760, son of Richard Dendy and Ann Caffyn, two families prominent in the history of the General Baptist Chapel in Worthing Road (see Emily Kensett's History of the Free Christian Church, Horsham, *published in 1921, and John Caffyn's* Sussex Believers - Baptist Marriages in the 17th and 18th Centuries, *published in 1988).   But Thomas might also belong to the Itchingfield family of Dendys, one of whom figures in a case of highway robbery in Chapter Five.*

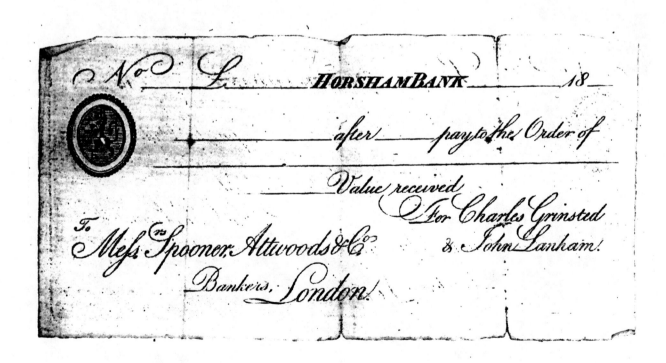

A Horsham Bank Note

Farthing Bridge - woodcut by Howard Dudley from *The History and Antiquities of Horsham*
(published 1836)

Footpads attacking a man - pen and wash drawing by Samuel Hieronymous Grimm (1773)

Horsham Museum MSS Cat. No. 452, *extracted by* **Norman Hewell**

William Longhurst	**for Highway Robbery of Peter Dendy**
Daniel Harwood	
Thomas Philpot	

Spring Assizes at Horsham – 9th March 1818

Mr Peter Dendy (a farmer who lived in Itchingfield) left Horsham Market in the Bishopric, near to midnight on Saturday 31st January 1818. By the time he reached Farthing Bridge it was 1st February and there he was stopped by two men who dragged him from his horse and picked his pockets. They took a pocket book which contained six one pound notes, being two Bank of England notes and the others were of the Dorking Bank, and a nankeen bag with key attached, which contained about six shillings. The book, bag and key here produced by the constable are confirmed to be those stolen. The night was very dark and he does not know the persons who robbed him. After the robbery, he remounted his horse, rode back to the Bishopric and there shouted a warning to others that he had been robbed. He then rode home to Itchingfield.

Statement by **William Durrant** – **21st February 1818**

He had been employed by **William Sandham Esq.** to (?) mud a pond on his farm in Horsham, on the road to Farthing Bridge, and he found in the pond the pocket book, bag and key now produced, which he took to the constable of Horsham, who had been, days before, searching for them as connected with Mr Dendy's robbery. He had found them on the previous Wednesday.

Statement by **Edmund Etherton** – **21st February 1818**

Edmund Etherton, a blacksmith, states that on Monday afternoon 9th February he saw **Thomas Philpot** of Horsham in his master's stable and he appeared to be very upset. He said to Philpot that he had heard about Mr Dendy's robbery and that he was afraid that it would be a bad job. The prisoner agreed but said *"Sooner than I will tell, I will be hanged".* Then he burst into tears and said that he feared that Harwood would tell and that therefore, he would tell first and that he should be taken as evidence for Mr Dendy, if he told it first. He then said that he with **Daniel Harwood** and **William Longhurst**, both of Horsham, labourers, when they attacked Mr Dendy on the highway near to Farthing Bridge on Saturday night. That Harwood and Longhurst stopped him and pulled him from his horse and picked his pockets of his pocket book, which contained very little – four one pound notes and six shillings and sixpence in coins and after they had robbed Mr Dendy, they heard him shouting in the Bishopric. Philpot wished Mr Etherton to write it down, but **Mr Whitmore**, Philpot's master, came and wrote it down and the informant signed it.

On Monday 9th February in the evening Longhurst and Harwood were arrested and taken to Horsham Gaol and Philpot was also taken to Horsham Gaol but later removed to Petworth House of Correction to keep him apart from the other two. Philpot had been told by Harwood that the pocket book, bag and key had been weighted with stones being tied to them and thrown into a pond on the Sandham farm in Horsham, where Harwood was employed.

Note. Evidently, Philpot was persuaded to give evidence for the Crown and the other prisoners were found guilty of Highway Robbery.

ဩ   Chapter Six - Murder or Manslaughter   ର

Horsham Museum MSS Cat. No. 456, *extracted by* ***Norman Hewell***

James Geere for Manslaughter of Thomas Searle

Midsummer Assizes at Lewes 7th August 1819

A warrant was issued by the Coroner for the arrest of **James Geere** as follows: -

To the constable of the hundred of Easewrithe in the said county and to all other peace officers within the same county and also to the keeper of the common gaol at Horsham in the said county whereas by an inquisition taken before me, one of His Majesty's coroners for the county of Sussex the day and year hereunder written. On view of the body of **Thomas Searle** lying dead at the parish of Storrington in the said county. James Geere, late of the parish of Storrington aforesaid, labourer, stands charged with feloniously killing and slaying of the said Thomas Searle.

These are therefore by virtue of office in His Majesty's name to charge and command you or any of you forthwith safely to convey the body of the said James Geere to His Majesty's said gaol at Horsham aforesaid and safely to deliver the same to the keeper thereof and these are likewise by virtue of my said office in His Majesty's name to will and require you the said keeper to received the body of the said James Geere into your custody and him safely to keep in the said gaol until he should be thence discharged by due course of law and for your so doing this is your warrant given under my hand and seal this 14th day of May 1819.   **J L Ellis,** Coroner

The case for the defence

The unfortunate young man, the object of this prosecution, was committed to prison on 14th May last under the coroner's warrant after the inquisition taken before him for feloniously killing Thomas Searle. The circumstances which led to the distressing event were as follows: -

On Storrington Fair day, the deceased and the prisoner - who were both slightly under the influence of liquor - were watching a battle with many other spectators. The deceased was offended by an expression used by the prisoner about the unfairness of a blow given by one of the combatants. The deceased insisted that the prisoner should fight him, but the prisoner refused, because they had been friends for such a long time. The deceased then struck the prisoner but he repeated that he would not fight. After a minute or two the deceased came and struck the prisoner again, urging him to fight but the prisoner still refused. Again the deceased came and struck a blow and stating that he would not be so used, he began to fight. The fight continued during the next quarter of an hour, during which the prisoner tried to stop the fight offering to treat the deceased. He, however, refused to listen and after about seven rounds, a severe struggle took place during which, the deceased's head was held under the prisoner's arm but he kept striking the prisoner in the side. The prisoner attempted to push the other away and they fell over, the prisoner falling on top. After a short time, the deceased was senseless. He was raised up, but died almost immediately.

Henry Turner and **Thomas White,** who were examined before the Coroner, will both give evidence at the prisoner's trial. They will confirm that the deceased and the prisoner have always been good friends and that the prisoner was unwilling to fight, despite the repeated provocation by the deceased. They will also confirm the prisoner's personal conduct and character when this dreadful happening occurred, and that he volunteered to attend the inquest without making any attempt to escape.

Mr Dennett and **Mr Byass** *(both surgeons of Storrington)* state that they do not attribute Thomas Searle's death to the blows which he had received, which were slight, but to his violent passions. One or both of these gentlemen will be at the prisoner's trial and will give evidence to the same effect and will also speak upon his personal good conduct.

Horsham Museum MSS 639, *extracted by* **John Hurd**

The King vs Henry James Hewett for the Murder of Edward Smith

Lent Assizes, Horsham 1830

Case for the defence of the Prisoner, Henry James Hewett

Henry James Hewett lived with his mother and father in Horsham. At about 7.30 on Saturday 6th March 1830 he went to the *Queen's Head*. There he saw **William Smithers,** a labourer of Horsham, and **Henry Harden** with several others who had *"lost 3 pots of beer"* playing cards. Hewett sat down and drank with them until **Edward Smith** came in and asked him and two others to play cards. They cut for partners and Hewett and Harden played against Smith and another man whose name he could not remember. After losing two or three games Smith got up and said he would not play any more doubles but challenged Hewett to play for a half gallon of beer. Hewett refused and continued playing with the others for several games. **Stephen Mitchell** challenged anyone in the house to play for sixpence and a pint of beer; **Thomas Woodman** accepted. Woodman played and lost and agreed to play again but through a *"false deal"* a disturbance commenced and Mitchell demanded the money: Woodman challenged Mitchell to a fight, which he accepted. The landlord sent for a Headborough (parish constable) to clear the house.

When they got into the street they commenced fighting - William Smithers seconded Mitchell, and Henry Hewett seconded Woodman. Hewett and Smithers were *"much intoxicated"*. Smithers said that if Hewett did not get out of the way he would knock him down; **John Heath,** a shoemaker, separated them. Hewett said that Mitchell was a coward and Woodman should fight him for five shillings. Smith asked Hewett *"Who is a coward!"* and offered to fight him for 5 shillings: Hewett declined. Smith pulled off his frock and offered to fight Hewett *and* his brother. **Mrs Hewett** said, *"You shall not hit either of them"* whereupon Smith struck her in the mouth and immediately turned and hit Henry Hewett until he fell with Smith on top of him.

William Smithers said that several people including Heath and Mitchell were drunk. Some 4 or five minutes after the first fight he looked round and saw that the Hewett brothers and Smith were fighting again. He saw Hewett stab Smith in the breast 3 or 4 times but could not actually see anything in his hand; Smith was striking Hewett. The evidence was divided about whether George was attempting to restrain his brother or to assist him against Smith. John Heath reported that **George Hewett** followed his brother and put his hands over his shoulders as if to stop him. Mitchell said *"I will have no unfair play"* and threw George down in the road. George spoke to his mother who was standing nearby and said that his hand was *"nearly cut off"*.

John Pierce picked Smith up but Smith told him *"I am stabbed in the side, let me lie down"*. Blood was coming from his neck. Pierce saw the clasp knife which Hewett held *"back handed"*. When Hewett got up he said, *"Bloody end to you! I'll have revenge on you somehow!"* Henry Harden took Hewett home. George Hewett arrived home at about the same time saying that his hand was nearly cut off - **Mrs Stephen Mitchell** said, *"It was that damn'd heath hook done it"*. Pierce had brought a heath hook which he sent home in Mrs Mitchell's basket after speaking to **John Hyatt.** At some point during the fight the hook was seen in Mitchell's hand.

When Henry Hewett got home he insisted on being searched which was done by Henry Harden and several others. His knife was taken from him but no blood was discovered. Mrs Mitchell came in again and reported that Smith was stabbed and dying. Hewett went to bed and remained there until **Henry Jordan** the constable came and took him to the coroner, where he was found guilty of wilful murder.

The Defence acknowledged the main facts but maintained that the fight was partly the result of passionate drunken behaviour and partly self defence. The Defence challenged the medical evidence provided by the surgeon **Mr Lovegrove** concerning the cause of death. The coroner concluded that a cut jugular vein was the cause of death and that Hewett had caused that injury. The Defence produced medical evidence that there were other wounds that were more likely to be the cause of death. There was more than one weapon at the scene and many people had joined in the scuffle including **John Chatfield** and **Henry Harding** who had knives - and John Pierce's furze hook.[7]

The document is endorsed with the information that Henry Hewett was found guilty of manslaughter and sentenced to transportation for life.

The Queen's Head, in Horsham, from an old postcard

Editorial comment. *This case is mentioned in William Albery's account of the murder, published in* Reminiscences of Horsham, *being the Recollections of Henry Burstow, in 1911. The relevant passage is on page 25. It includes a detail not included in the case for the defence - that Hewett's mother urged him on in his fight with Edward Smith. Burtow's claim that Hewett retuned to Horsham after ten years is not borne out by the 1841 Horsham census - the only Hewett shown in that was Eliza Hewett, aged 28, who lived in Sussex Row in East Street with her daughter Harriett, aged 9, and a James Hewett, aged 14, who was a servant living in the Carfax. Henry Burstow said of the case:*

"I can also recollect hearing my brothers and sisters talking of a murder committed on Saturday, 8th March, 1830, at the "Queen's Head" Inn. Several young men were inside that house drinking and card playing when, late at night, they fell out among themselves. The landlord turned them outside, when two of them, Harry Hewett and Edward Smith, resumed the quarrel. After fighting a few minutes, Hewett took out a knife and stabbed Smith, who died in consequence after about a quarter of an hour. In the small crowd round the two fighters were Hewett,s mother, Charlotte Venn, and brother. The mother egged on her son to fight, "give it to him, Harry" she cried, "have your revenge" but the brother tried to get the knife away, and in doing so had his hand cut very badly. Hewett was lodged in Horsham Gaol to await his trial at the coming Horsham Assizes.... At the last Horsham Assizes, held on 30 March, 1830, the charge of murder was preferred, but Hewett was found guilty of manslaughter only. He was sentenced to transportation to life, but came back to Horsham after the expiration of ten years of his sentence."

---

[7] *The Return Of The Native* , by- Thomas Hardy,. There is a good description of a furze-hook in Chapter 5 - *The Journey across the Heath; On coming in her turn to each of these spots she found half a dozen long limp brambles which he had cut from the bush during his halt and laid out straight beside the path. They were evidently intended for furze-faggot bonds which he meant to collect on his return. ...... By the door lay Clym's furze-hook and the last handful of faggot-bonds she had seen him gather; they had plainly been thrown down there as he entered the house.*

Full Particulars

OF A MOST

Wilful Murder,

COMMITTED AT

HORSHAM,

On Saturday night last, about 11 o'clock, on the Body of a person named Smith, during a scuffle, which originated from a dispute respecting a game at Cards, at a Public House, called the Queen's Head Inn.

A most Wilful and Diabolical Murder took place in the town of Horsham, on Saturday night last, 6 inst. under the following circumstances. It appears that George Hewert, Henry Hewert, and Smith, had been playing together at cards, on the above night, at the Queen's Head, when, about eleven o'clock, a dispute arose, and Henry Hewert and the deceased went into the street and fought. After a short contest, in which Smith appeared to have the advantage, George Hewert drew his knife, and attempted to stab Smith, which Henry Hewert perceiving, endeavoured to prevent, and in doing so his hand was very severely cut. Henry then went away to have his hand dressed, and as soon as he was gone a struggle commenced between George Hewert and Smith, when the latter received a dreadful wound in the neck. Smith had only time to request some person to send for medical assistance, before he dropped down and expired. It is said that George Hewert afterwards very deliberately wiped the blood from off the weapon, and that the mother of the Hewerts was present during the struggle. Both Hewerts were afterwards taken into custody. A Coroner's Inquest was held at the King's head, on the body of Smith, last Monday, when a verdict of Wilful Murder was returned against George Hewert, but Henry, Hewert was liberated. Smith was a young Man about 19 years of age.

From the Cheap and Expeditious Press, 21 North-street, Brighton.

Broadsheet concerning the murder of Edward Smith (HM MSS Cat. No. 5147)

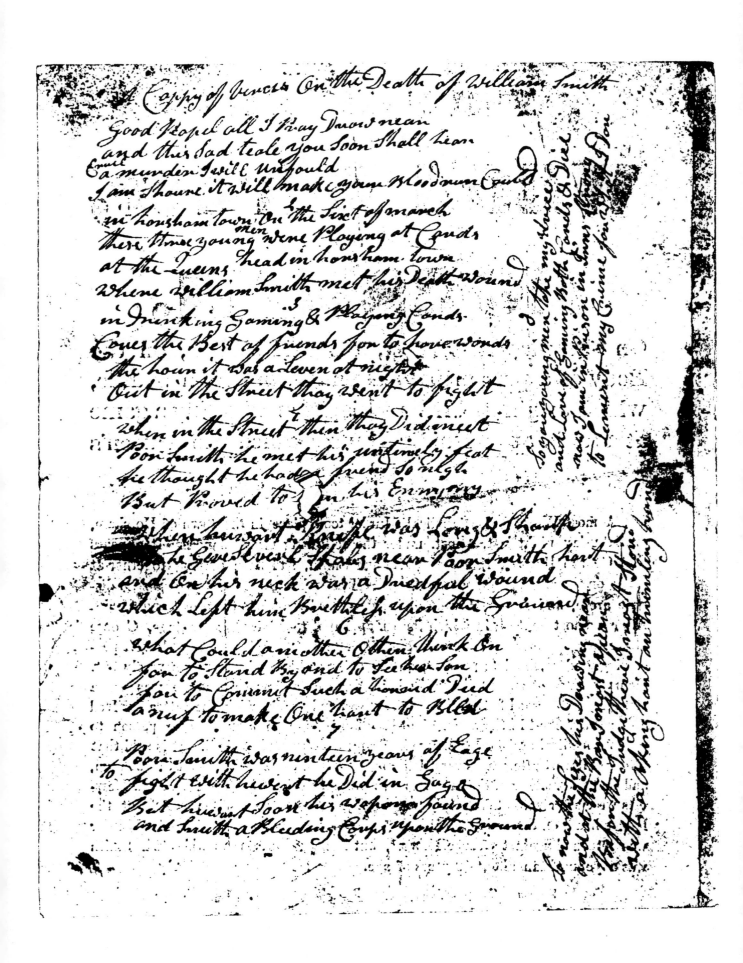

A Coppy off verces On the Death of William Smith

Good People all I Pray Draw near
and this Sad teale you Soon Shall hear
a murder I will unfould
I am Shoure it will make your Blood run Could

in horsham town On the Sixt off march
there three young men were Ployeing at Cards
at the Queens head in horsham town
where william Smith met his death wound

in Drinking Gaming & Playing Cards
Coues the Best of friends for to have words
the houre it was aleven at night
Out in the Street thay went to fight

when in the Street then thay Did meet
Poor Smith he met his untimely feat
he thought he had a freind so nigh
But Proved to be his Enimy

when laussant Knife was Long & Sharp
he Gave several Stabs near Poor Smith hart
and On her neck was a Dredful wound
which Left him Breathless upon the Ground

what Could a mother Othen think On
for to Stand By and to See her Son
for to Commit Such a Vivard Ded
is nuf to make One heart to Bleed

Poor Smith was nineteen years of Eage
fight with he did in Rage
But hewist Soon his wepons found
and Smith a Bleeding Corps upon the Ground

Manuscript copy of verses on the death of Edward Smith, on the back of the broadsheet

Horsham Museum has now acquired a broadsheet, HM MSS Cat. No. 5147, *which gives details of the murder, but appears to confuse the two Hewett brothers; George was said to be responsible for the murder, not Henry Hewett, and the verdict was not* "wilful murder" *but* "manslaughter". *The broadsheet was printed in Brighton, and this suggests that there was a well-established market for this kind of publication. It would be interesting to know who was the entrepreneur behind the* "Cheap and Expeditious Press".

On the other side of the broadsheet are A Coppy of Verses On the Death of William Smith, *in manuscript. These verses have an awkward charm. We can imagine them being declaimed with appropriate dramatic emphasis in kitchens and public houses within days or even hours of the event. Spelling and punctuation are as written.*

A Coppy of Verses On the Death of William Smith

Good Peopel all I Pray Draw near
and this sad teale you soon shall hear
a Cruel murder I will unfould
I am shoure it will make your Blood run Could
in horsham town on the Sixth of March
there ?three/?these young men were Playing at Cards
at the Queens Head in horsham town
Where William Smith met his Death Wound
in Drinking Gaming & Playing Cards
Comes the Best of friends for to have words
the hour it was a Leven at night
Out in the Street they went to fight
When in the Street then they Did meet
Poor Smith hee met his untimely fate
he thought he had a friend so nigh
But Proved to be his Enurmy
When huwarts knife was long & sharp
he gave severl stabs near poor Smith's heart
and on his neck was a Dreadful Wound
which left him brethless upon the Ground
what could a mother O then think on
for to stand by and to see her son
for to Commit such a horerd Deed
a nuf to make One hart to Bleed
Poor Smith was ninteen years of Eage
to fight with hewert he Did in Gage
But huwart soon his wepon found
and Smith a Bleeding Corps upon the Ground
So now the Sizes his Drawing near
and at the Bar I most apear
Befor the Judge there I most stand
with a aking hart an tremling hand
So you young men take my advice
and Lave of Gaming Both Cards & Dice
now I am in Prison in Irns strong
to Lament my Crime for what I Don.

These are similar to the verses quoted by Albery, and known by Henry Burstow, but this version is clearly written by someone more familiar with spelling, grammar, rhyme and metre. Burstow's version is as follows - it may be felt to lack the pathos and directness of the original version;

At the "Queen's Head ", Inn in Horsham Town,
Poor Edward Smith met his death wound:
Drinking and gaming, and playing at cards,
Causes the best of friends to have words.

Drinking and gaming till twelve at night,
The out into the street they went to fight;
Poor Smith thought he'd a friend so nigh,
But proved to be an enemy.

Young Hewett with his knife so sharp,
Aimed several times at poor Smith's heart,
He gave one stab, such a horrid deed,
Enough to make one's heart to bleed.

What could a mother be thinking on,
To stand near by and see her son
Engage in wicked, deadly strife,
And rob his poor young friend of life.

The Horsham Assizes now draw near,
And at the bar Hewett must appear,
Before the Judge he must now stand,
With aching heart, and trembling hand.

Young men! Take warning by his plight,
Shun drink and cards ny day and night,
Be honest sober, kind and free,
And so avoid such misery.

Boys Fighting

Boys fighting, Bowes and Carver

Horsham Museum MSS 524, *extracted by **John Hurd***

The Queen (on prosecution of William Gibson) vs John Payne for Murder

1851 Sussex Assizes at Lewes

The indictment says that the prisoner, *"not having the fear of God before his eyes, but being moved and seduced by the Devil ....with force & arms......did make an assault.........*(on Saturday 14th June)*.......upon one William Gibson the younger..........with a certain knife of the value of sixpence.........in his left hand....... into right side of the chest between 8th & 9th ribs....did strike and thrust...giving one mortal wound......half an inch wide and two inches deep...from which William Gibson died on 25th June"*

John Payne aged 11
William Gibson aged 13

No witnesses. Defendant stated that *"the deceased hit him aside of his head with his fist".*

(William) Stedman for prosecution : small knife passed to police by prisoner's mother

The case for the defence

Henry Vaughan (assistant sexton) lives at mother's house adjacent to the house of Mrs. Elms, mistress of Lucy Jenkins, and opposite the bakehouse. *(Mrs Elms lived at what is now no. 28 in the Causeway - the bakehouse opposite was that of Thomas Dendy in nos. 19/20).*

Returning home at about 8 pm, after the event, he found **Robert Killick,** the prisoner (John Payne) and the deceased (William Gibson) talking together; on Gibson saying that Payne had stabbed him, he replied that he did not mean to do it. Killick said that he would be hanged or transported; Payne turned pale and began to cry. Gibson went towards his father's house near the almshouses beyond the church *(in Normandy).*

Thomas Sadler (in service with Mrs. Fuller of Warnham Court)

While on his way to visit his parents who lived near the almshouses: he stepped to speak to **George Gates**, servant to Mr. Plumer, at Mr Plumer's house. On continuing he saw the two boys; Gibson going towards church stopped & spoke to *(the Rev.)* Mr. Hodgson's servant at the Vicarage gate, then continued; Payne, coming towards Town, stopped at the bakehouse or Mr Dendy's door, then he saw him running towards his parents' house. Sadler caught up with Gibson near the Church; he was crying and holding his hand to his side. *"What is the matter, my man?"* *"Oh we was only throwing stones"* and he said that Payne was sharpening a knife and ran it into him.

John Philpott (Master of the National School)

Payne was his pupil from Midsummer 1845-1850: he was of meek disposition, good tempered, kind and friendly to school fellows, never cruel or aggressive to other boys

The Rev. Robert Ashdowne (Minister of Baptist Church & schoolmaster)

Taught Payne from 1850-1851. Spoke of him in same terms as Mr. Philpot.

(Written on outside of document) Verdict: Manslaughter. Transportation for 10 years (?from Parkhurst)

❧ Chapter Seven - Nuisance and nightsoil ❧

Horsham Museum MSS Cat. No. 343, *extracted by Norman Hewell*

Richard Thornton – Schoolmaster – for disposal of nightsoil upon Gaol Green

Summer Assizes at Horsham on Friday 11th July 1788

The case for the prosecution

On 2nd October, Tuesday, in the morning **Richard Thornton** caused a prodigious amount of dung, human excrement and filth to be poured upon Gaol Green. This mess remained there until Tuesday 9th October, when it was removed but a nasty smell remained for about another fortnight. This was not the first time that this happened and he had previously been charged and fined forty shillings at the Midsummer Sessions for 1787. *(Richard Thornton was Headmaster of Thornton's Academy, a boys' school on in the north side of the Carfax. The school was in the Old Gaol, which had been built in 1640, and the Carfax was still known at that time as Gaol Green. An earlier Gaol had been built along North Street, and the Gaoler's house associated with this Gaol was on the corner of the Carfax and North Street, so the Gaol had been in this vicinity for a long time).*

It seems that Thornton had a habit of doing this when the two (parish) constables were absent, attending the Assizes, with the mistaken idea that if it was not noticed till after it had been removed, he should be free from punishment. Although the nightsoil was from three houses, it was reckoned that he should be capable of disposing of it safely by night, but in his defence, he stated that the only alternative was to tip it on his school-yard. This muck caused such a nuisance and obstruction, let alone the smell, that riders, coaches, carts and carriages were unable to pass that way, pedestrians had to hold their noses with their handkerchiefs and residing neighbours were caused great distress. The inhabitants in the defendant's neighbourhood were now in hopes that they would be able to live in wholesome and pure air. It is hoped that he may be so punished on the present conviction that he may be deterred from committing a like offence in the future.

Witnesses to be called for the prosecution

Edward Joanes and **Francis Passell** emptied eighty buckets of dung, excrement and filth upon Gaol Green by direction of the defendant.

Nicholas Whitman and **Peter Caven**, the two Horsham Constables, witness that the muck was on Gaol Green from 2nd October till 9th October.

Mrs Elizabeth Draper *(widow of Captain Draper)* lives next door and the muck remained almost opposite to her house from 2nd October till 9th October and the smell was such a nuisance that it operated as an emetic upon her and her family. Many persons passing that way were forced to hold their noses with their handkerchiefs and turn to go another way. For about a fortnight after it was removed, the effluvia it left was almost intolerable. She had to keep her windows closed.

Mrs Eleanor Hammond *(wife of the landlord of the* Lamb Inn, *on the corner of the Carfax and London Road)* lived next door to Mrs Draper and was pregnant and almost far enough advanced to take to her bed. The windows of her house do not close properly shut and after being very tired, after running her inn, she lay awake for many nights on account of the smell. She was continually being sick, and she complained to the defendant, who replied that he agreed about the smell and that it was very bad for the neighbourhood and that he would not have done it had it not been for Mrs Draper!

Mr John Aldridge, an acting local magistrate, saw the nuisance and together with other magistrates sent for the defendant to come to them at the *King's Head* on Saturday 6th October last to discuss the subject. The defendant behaved with great insolence and justified his conduct by saying that he had every right to do what he had.

Mr William Ellis, Clerk of the Peace for Sussex, to prove the previous conviction and fine of forty shillings (£2.00) at the Midsummer Sessions 1787, from the records.

Since preparing the list of witnesses to be called, Edward Joanes and Francis Passell have been sent out of the way, by the defendant, but it is thought that the evidence of James Vinall will suffice.

James Vinall was called upon by the defendant to bring a quantity of mould to mix with the muck and carry it away. On Sunday night, Monday night and Tuesday morning, the 7th, 8th and 9th October 1787 helped by his servant, they filled his dung cart and took away the muck from opposite the defendant's premises on Gaol Green.

Richard Thornton was convicted and fined. On 16th January 1789 he sent a note to the prosecution saying that he was ready to pay. Presumably he could not afford the fine in July 1788, but six months later he had moved away from Horsham and had enough. Whether he has sold the premises or raised the money in some other way, we do not know.

Editorial comment:. It is strange that Richard Thornton is said to have "moved away" from Horsham, because his school was still there when he died in 1814 - though by then his son James was running it. It may be that he simply moved away from Horsham for a while, leaving James to run the school. Richard Thornton is known to have had property in Brighton - the Star and Garter Inn - which is mentioned in a draft case (HM MSS Cat No. 288.103) and his will (HM MSS Cat. No. 2327). He is known to have lived at Mickleham, near Dorking, before he came to Horsham. This case is all the more surprising and difficult to comprehend, because Thornton was a person of considerable standing in the town. He had served as one of the Bailiffs of the Borough in 1781, when he would have been responsible for the keeping of law and order in the town. But it does seem, from other references to him, that he could be arrogant and short-tempered. It seems quite likely that he may have been the schoolmaster referred to in the case of slander! (see Chapter Nine)

NIGHT CART.

Cart removing nightsoil, Bowes and Carver

Interior of a public house - George Cruikshank in *Sketches by Boz* (1836)

Horsham Museum MSS Cat. No. 504, *extracted by Norman Hewell*

The Queen vs William Passell and Henry Heath for felonious administration of Cantharides (Spanish Fly) *(Spanish Fly is used as a diuretic and an aphrodisiac for horses)*

Spring Assizes at Lewes – 16ᵗʰ March 1840

The case for the defence of the prisoner Henry Heath

Henry Heath faces two charges;
1. A charge for feloniously administering cantharides (Spanish Fly) with intent to poison or to inflict some grievous bodily harm.
2. A charge, arising out of the same transaction, for a misdemeanour at the Common Law.

Heath is a carrier, having carried on that business at and in the neighbourhood of Horsham very punctually and industriously during many years. The case against him lies mainly in the evidence of the chemist, **Mr Snelling**, referring to Heath's purchase of the cantharides for a legitimate purpose (treating a stallion). The fact of this purchase is indisputable and consequently, the drug used must have come from Heath's hands, even assuming the guilt of the other accused party. Heath is also unable to prove that, on leaving the chemist's shop, the two packets of drugs which he had purchased were delivered to Passell. It remains to consider the other points of evidence, which it is confidently submitted are strong, if not convincing, on Heath's behalf. These points are as follows:-

1. That Passell made the gin & beer potions without Heath's intervention.
2. That Heath drank it and was ill and that Passell did not drink it and made an excuse to go away although he was the person who ordered and might therefore be expected to partake of it.

Note   It would appear that it was normal for a drink of Gin & Beer to be taken hot, presumably as a toddy, and the beer was poured into a warming mug and put on the fire to heat up. The gin was then mixed in later.

Some observations might be made upon the gross conduct of Passell in attempting to tamper with the witness, **Mathews**, to foreswear himself for the purpose of involving a fellow prisoner, as also in the line of defence he chose to take on his examination before the committing magistrate, with a similar object; but Heath has no wishes to retaliate in this respect, save as may be necessary to establish circumstances tending to relieve himself from a very serious charge, and as those circumstances are material to his own defence. With respect to the first count of the charge against the two prisoners, there does not seem room to apprehend that any attempt will be made to support it. It is hoped that the jury may be induced to consider Heath innocent of participation in the crime alleged against him and. as he has always hitherto maintained a good character for honesty and integrity, that so he may be restored to his original position in the estimation of his fellow townsmen and neighbours.

Examinations taken upon oath before me, **(Robert Henry Hurst),** one of her Majesty's Justices of the Peace, in and for the said county this 15ᵗʰ day of February 1840 in the presence and hearing of William Passell charged with felony.

George Cheesman of Horsham in the County of Sussex, Ostler, on his oath saith

On Monday evening 3ʳᵈ February, I was in the *Anchor Tap* bar between eight and nine o'clock. There were a dozen or fifteen persons, Henry Heath and William Passell came in, Heath sat down between me and Henry Vowls. Passell remained standing close to the door. He ordered a pint of gin and beer of the landlady Sarah Charman. She drew the beer and said to Passell *"you had better come in here and make it. There is no candle and very little fire in the other room"*. He said *"no, I will go into the other room and make it"*. He took the beer and went into the other room. Henry Heath got up and went to the door of the other room. He returned directly. About a minute later, Passell came into the room with a mug in his hand, Henry Heath took the mug from him and drank, Passell offered it to Heath. Heath then gave the mug to me and I drank. I then said to Passell *"What have you here?"* He replied *"Nothing but a few wood ashes and that will not hurt you".* The gin and beer was very thick and I would have a fresh mug. I got a clean mug and poured out the gin and beer into it. I placed the mug in which it had been, on the shelf. I then drank again and gave it to Henry Heath and he drank. He then gave it to Vowls who drank. Passell said to Heath *"I am going out for a few minutes, I shall be back directly".* I think he called Heath by his name. He went but did not return and he did not pay for the gin and beer. The mug was left on the shelf and on Tuesday morning the 4th February, I and Henry Vowls took it to Mr Herring the chemist.

In the night of Monday and about two o'clock as I believe, I was seized with violent pain and I continued in pain during the night. I looked at the pot and finding something at the sides which I was satisfied was not wood ashes, I took it to Mr Herring. The pot now produced is the same one that Passell mixed the gin and beer in which I put on the shelf. Heath did not order anything. Passell gave the order for the gin and beer as soon as he came into the room. He did not remain longer than it took to draw the beer. Heath remained ten minutes before he went to the door of the other room. Several of the persons were sitting round the fire place, but there was plenty of room to come to the fire to make gin and beer. I never knew any person make it in the other room. Heath went out of my sight, but I do not think he had time to go to the fire place in the other room. The pot was nearly full when Heath drank. When he gave it to me I think not more than a beer glass full had been drank. Passell did not drink at all in my presence or ever offered to drink. I will swear that Passell said he would return in a few minutes.

Heath came into the tap on Tuesday morning. He had something to drink. He said he was very ill. I drank three times from the pot. I will swear that I never knew any thing being put into beer before at the Anchor tap. I do not remember that Heath was at the tap last Saturday, I have not had conversation with Heath on this subject. Heath has not given me money or anything or asked me to say nothing about it or promised it.

Sworn before me Robert Henry Hurst   Signed George Cheesman

(all the following statements are similarly sworn and signed, but Eliza Garman, Sarah Charman, Henry Vowls and John Mathews signed with a mark).

Eliza Garman of Horsham in the county of Sussex, Singlewoman on her oath saith

I live with my sister Sarah Charman who keeps the *Anchor Tap*. I was there on Monday evening the 3rd February. When I first saw William Passell, he was in the tap room, he had a mug in his hand and asked me to drink, it was gin and beer. I refused but I afterwards drank. He asked me a second time and I drank again. The mug now produced is the same as I drank out of. Passell went out and I afterwards went out into the town. I returned about nine o'clock and he was not there. I was taken ill in the night and have been ill since. I am under the care of Mr Lovegrove. I had been out before I drank and when I returned, Master Heath was in the bar. I did not see Heath go out. I saw Passell in the tap and John Mathews was there. I was not in the bar all the time. Mathews was eating his supper but there was no light in the room except from the fire. I saw Passell put some chips on. I was not in bad health before that night. I first saw Passell in the room blowing the fire, the beer was on the fire.

Joseph Lovegrove of Horsham aforesaid, Surgeon, on his oath saith

I have attended Eliza Garman and was first called to her on Wednesday evening 5th February. She was at the *Anchor Tap*. On my arrival the symptoms I found were pallid countenance, cold clammy sweats, severe pain and heat on the stomach and bowels, nausea and vomiting, small and frequent pulse, frequent and almost constant desire to pass urine with liability to do it accompanied by a bloody discharge. Having ascertained the nature of these symptoms, I asked her if she had been partaking of something out of a mug which was then in the room. I looked at the mug which is the same now produced and was satisfied that it was Spanish Fly. I examined the paper in the mug on which there was also Spanish Fly. There was now eight to ten grains remaining in the mug. It is a very dangerous drug and is imported. There is an insect called Spanish Fly in this country, but it is not used as a drug. I was satisfied from the symptoms and the examination of the mug that Eliza Garman had taken Spanish Fly. It is so powerful, that I have known violent effects arise from one grain. I have prescribed for her and she has been under my care. She has been very ill. It was the appearance on the side of the mug of having been mixed with the beer. A sediment may have taken place by pouring from one mug to another. I think the larger portion was taken with the beer than is now in the mug. I have kept it since I saw it at the Tap.

Francis Snelling of Horsham aforesaid, Chemist on his oath saith

On Monday evening 3rd February William Passell came to my shop and stated that he wanted some horse powders, the same as he had been accustomed to have, and that a friend of his also wanted some. Henry Heath and a man of the name of Bennett who were unknown to me at that time, came into the shop when Passell was there. The horse powders were made up and Heath then asked if I had any Spanish Fly. I asked him the object of his enquiry and he replied that he had a stallion which he wished to work this season. Passell said that was the fact. I asked the question because Spanish Fly is a dangerous drug and it is invariably my custom not to let a stranger have it. I then asked Heath if he would have the powder or the Fly? He asked to see the Fly, which I then produced. He then said he would have the powder as well and asked for half an ounce which I supplied him with. I handed the Fly to Heath with one parcel of powders. Both Passell and Heath put money on the counter. I laid the change on the counter and they divided it. They all left the shop together, it was about eight o'clock. Passell did not ask for Spanish Fly and if Heath had come for it alone then I would not have let him have it. I have since ascertained that Heath has a stallion.

Sarah wife of **Richard Charman** of Horsham aforesaid, Housekeeper on her oath saith

My husband keeps the Anchor Tap, I recollect Monday evening the 3rd February Henry Heath came in first and Passell followed him. I was standing at the bar door, Passell ordered a pint of gin and beer. I drew it and was about to put it on the fire in the bar. He said *"I would rather make it myself in the other room"*. I told him there was no light and very little fire. He said *"you attend to your business, I would rather make it myself"*. I took the warming mug in one hand and the mug now produced in the other. I had drawn the beer in it. I went with him into the tap room. Passell took the warming mug from me with the beer in it and put it on the fire. I took the mug now produced and went into the bar for the gin and sugar and I returned into the tap room with it. I said to Passell *"Shall I mix it?"* He said *"no, I would rather mix it myself, attend to your own business"*. Henry Heath was sitting with George Cheesman who asked him where the gin and beer was which he had been speaking of? Heath *said "I will go and see!"* Heath went to the Tap room door and asked Passell if the gin and beer was hot. He answered *"I am just coming!"* Henry Charman was in the room with John Mathews. I saw Passell take the mug from Charman, he came with it into the passage and asked me to drink, twice, and I refused. I gave the warming pot to Passell, I looked at it after Passell had used it and, observing something in it, I washed it before I used it again. I saw the fire blazing. I am quite certain Heath did not go to the fire where the beer was warmed. No person could go into the Tap without I saw him. It was not customary for persons to mix their own gin and beer. Heath came into the Tap last Saturday and stayed about an hour I did not see Passell drink. The warming mug was turned up on the hob.

James Herring of Horsham aforesaid, Chemist on his oath saith

The witness George Cheesman and Henry Vowls came to my shop on Tuesday morning 4th February, they brought the mug now produced, which was then moist. I wrote my name on the piece of paper now produced and gave the mug to Cheesman. I was satisfied that it was Spanish Fly.

Examinations continued, taken on oath this 17th day of February 1840 in the presence and hearing of William Passell and Henry Heath.

Francis Snelling of Horsham aforesaid, Chemist on his oath further saith

I do not recollect that William Passell asked the price of Spanish Fly. The price of it was asked, I think, by Heath and I do not recollect that Passell asked any question about the Spanish Fly. I do not recollect that each paid for it or what money each put down. I collected all the money laid on the counter and gave the change. When Heath told me the purpose for which he wanted the Spanish Fly, I referred to Passell to know if that was the truth. He did not state voluntarily that it was, before I referred to him.

Henry Vowls of Horsham aforesaid, Hairdresser on his oath saith

I was at the Anchor Tap on Monday evening the 3rd February. I saw Henry Heath and William Passell come in. Heath came into the bar and I got up from my chair to let him sit down. The witness George Cheesman sat on the other side. I heard Passell ask for a pint of gin and beer. After Mrs Charman drew the beer I saw Passell go to the tap room. Henry Heath got up about ten minutes later and went towards the tap room. He was out of my sight. I heard him ask if the gin and beer was ready. Passell said that he was just coming and Heath came back immediately, followed by Passell with the mug now produced in his hand. As soon as Heath had sat down Passell entered and I think that not more than a minute had passed. Heath was not away more than a minute and he did not have time to walk to the fire place and back. Passell gave the mug to Heath first who I believe drank some and then passed the mug to Cheesman, the mug was not quite full when Passell brought it in. After Cheesman had drank, he poured the gin and beer into another mug. I heard him ask Passell what was in it and he answered that a few wood ashes had blown into it. Cheesman put the mug now produced onto the shelf. Cheesman took a drink from the clean mug and gave it back to Heath, who put it to his mouth, but whether or not he had a drink I do not know. Heath then asked me if I would have any. I drank and passed it to Cheesman who drank again. He gave the mug to Heath who said to me *"Here Harry, you may drink this if you like, and we will have a pint hotter"*. It looked so thick that I tossed it under the grate. I heard Passell say that he was going and would be back presently. He did not drink in my presence and he did not return.

I was taken ill in the night and on Tuesday morning I went with Cheesman to Mr Herring's the chemist. I saw Passell and Heath together on Tuesday about half past twelve, near Piper's shop. I asked them if they would come down to the Anchor Tap, because they were wanted, that the girl was ill and so was Cheesman and so am I. Passell asked what made me ill and I said *"it was the Spanish Fly which one of you put into the beer!"* Passell said *"go along you D....D fool, it is something else you have been drinking, it never hurt me at all!"* Heath then said to Passell *"We had better go down"*. Passell said *"I shaln't go!"* Heath said *"I will come down as soon as I have had my dinner"*. I told Passell that if he did not come, he would be forced to come and he laughed at me. I am positive that Heath was not gone a minute from the bar. I did not lose sight of the mug from the time it was put into Heath's hand. I am certain that nothing was put into the mug after it was brought into the room. I will swear that nothing was put in, in my presence. I am not certain whether I said *"one of you"* or *"you put in the beer"*.

I went to the Tap on Tuesday morning about six o'clock, I remained ill for three or four days. I drank twice. When the second pot of gin and beer was made on Monday evening, Cheesman and Heath drank and I had some. That was mixed by Mrs Charman. A pint pot would generally go round several times with three or four in company. I know Passell was ill once and that he went to hospital. I shaved him twice a week when he was confined to his house. No offer was made to me to make it up. I have drank with Heath once since the 3rd February and that is the only time! The mug was quite full when it was brought into the bar. About half a quartern was gone. When I saw Passell and Heath together on Tuesday, Heath did not tell me that he was ill. George Piper, Henry Jenkins and a young man of the name of Reid were in Piper's shop.

John Mathews of Horsham aforesaid on his oath saith

I am under ostler at the Anchor. On Monday evening 3rd February, I was in the tap room alone for a while. William Passell came in with a pot in his hand and he was going to make some gin and beer on the fire. There was not much fire and it was pretty nigh out. There was some chips on the fire place. Henry Charman came in. About ten minutes later, Henry Heath came to the door but not into the room and said *"Is not this nearly ready?"* Passell said *"It is!"* I went out of the room and when I returned, no person was in the room. I did not see Heath go to the fire place. He might have gone without my seeing him perhaps. I saw him just against the door. I never saw him come in. When I went out Passell and Harry Charman were the only persons in the room. I saw Passell on Wednesday 12th February. I was coming from the Gaol and saw him near Monnery's corner. He called to me and said *"John, I want to speak to you"*. I asked what for and he said *"Will you swear that Mr Heath was in the tap that night and I will satisfy you"*. I said *"I know nothing about it, it is no concern of mine"*. I had no conversation with Passell before I told him that Heath was not in the tap. I will swear I had no conversation with Passell in the tap on the subject since Monday 3rd February. I do not know that I have told any person that Heath was standing by the fire place. Passell was sitting down, blowing the fire. He asked me to come and give evidence for him. I said I had no business here. He said he would pay me if I would swear that Heath was standing by the fire place. If I would come and give evidence, he would pay me. I was sitting in the tap room eating my supper. Passell continued using the bellows. I did not see him put anything into the beer. I was sitting with my back to Passell. What he said to me was "Will you swear that Heath was in the tap room that night" and I said *"I know nothing about it, I shall have no hand with it at all"*. He said *"If you do, I will satisfy you"*. Then he said *"I will see about that"*. I made no answer. He did not say *"I will satisfy you for your loss of time"*.

Henry Charman of Horsham aforesaid, Postboy on his oath saith

I was in the tap room at the Anchor on Monday evening the 3rd February. When I went in Passell was there. There was the warming pot on the fire with some gin and beer in. Mrs Charman came in and asked Passell if she should make it. He said *"No I can, you go and mind the other room!"* Passell took the pot off the fire when it was warm enough and mixed it by pouring from one pot to another. He asked me to drink, which I did, and I gave the pot into Passell's hand. He tipped the crib which was in the warming pot into the pint and Harry Heath came to the tap room door and asked if the gin and beer was ready. There was no light in the room, except from the fire. Passell said *"Yes, here it is"*. I was at the fire place and Heath did not come further than the door. He turned round directly and Passell followed him.

Men lying down, W.H. Pyne (*Etchings of Rustic Figures*)

๛ Chapter Nine - Rape ൠ

Horsham Museum MSS Cat. No. 319, *extracted by* **Norrman Hewell**

The King vs Thomas Ansell Junior for attempted Rape of Martha Baytupp

Midsummer Sessions 1783

The indictment says that *"Thomas Ansell the younger, late of Horsham, tanner, on 12ᵗʰ May ...in and upon Martha Baytupp, spinster in the Peace of God and our said Lord the King ... did make an assault ...and did beat wound and ill-treat her so that her Life was greatly despaired of with an Intent ... feloniously to ravish and carnally to know and other wrongs... to the great damage of the said Martha Baytupp and against the Peace of our said Lord the King his Crown and Dignity".*

Notes on cover; Brief - Mr. Courthopp. Medwin

The case for the prosecution.

On May 12th 1783 a May Fair was being held on Maplehurst Common. At about 7 pm **Martha Baytupp** of Nuthurst, a single lady working in the service of **Mr John Pollard**,[8] arrived at the fair. When she had been there for about half an hour, she was approached by a young man who she did not know, but has since found that his name was **Thomas Ansell** and that he was a tanner from Horsham, who said that he would go along with her. Four times she refused him, but he continued to pester her, pulling her about.   When she tried to get away from him to go home, he pulled her away from the fair, behind a wood pile and there he left her. She immediately began to run down Maplehurst Common towards her home. She had almost reached a house upon the common, where Mrs Steer lived, when she was overtaken by Thomas Ansell who put his arm round her waist and said he would take her home. She insisted that she wished to go alone, but he stayed with her. When they had walked about 110 yards from where he had overtaken her, they came to a copse. He asked her how much further it was to her home, and she pointed to a farmhouse where she was in service and insisted that he did not accompany her any further.   They argued for some time until he said *"You come down here into this copse with me"*, she said that she would not and she begged and pleaded with him to let her go home. He then dragged her, picked her up and carried her about 50 yards into the copse to a place between a brook and a bog where he threw her on to the ground and knelt on her stomach. She struggled violently and after some time she managed to get free, with him underneath, but he grabbed both her arms. She pleaded with him again to let her go, but he said he would be damned if she should go and that he would keep her all night unless she let him have his will. She continued to struggle, but he threw her down for a second time and pulled her petticoats up and his breeches down. He then knelt on her stomach and breasts, but she, being strong in the arms, prevented him from getting down upon her.

After some minutes, with the help of some hazel boughs, she managed to pull herself up and threw him off. He turned immediately and threw her down for a third time, almost into the brook. He let her get up, to avoid falling into the brook, but before she could get to her feet, he threw her down again. She had been screaming since the start and finding that she was almost exhausted and that she must soon let him have his way, she made a final effort and screamed as loud as she could.

Three gentlemen from Nuthurst were passing that way and heard the scream. She cried with relief when **Henry Linfield, Jonathan Bourne** and **Charles Flint** entered the copse and ran towards her. Ansell rolled into the brook, crept through a thick white thorn bush and up the bank into a clearing, Linfield and Flint backtracked to the lane where they met Ansell and caught him.   They asked him if he was not ashamed of himself and he answered *"No, but I will see you tomorrow"*. Whereupon he made off

---

[8]   John Pollard is listed in the 1785 Land tax for Nuthurst, in the south part of the parish, but the name of the farm he occupied is not given. Sussex Record Society, Vol. 82, *West Sussex Land Tax,* p. 169.

towards his horse which was tied a short distance away, mounted and galloped off home. Jonathan Bourne stayed with Martha, comforted her and gathered up her clothes. Her stays were half untied, both her petticoats were off, with both strings off the upper one. She could not find her cap and bonnet and her handkerchief was torn and hung down her back. She put her apron round her head and returned with Jonathan Bourne to the fair, where her aunt Spooner lived, she sells ale at fairs. Her aunt advised her to go directly to her Governor *(presumably Mr. Pollard)*, which she did that same evening and told him all that had happened.   The following day she found her stomach and back were very bruised and black and she felt so ill that she could not work without the help of her mistress.   She went with her father to visit **Mr Aldridge** *(John Aldridge of New Lodge, Horsham, M.P. for New Shoreham and a magistrate)* to obtain redress and she was sick and almost fainted. The next day Mr Aldridge granted a warrant to apprehend Ansell. This was directed to Flint and Bourne who apprehended him on the same day. *(Presumably Flint and Bourne were the parish constables of Nuthurst)*

It appears that **Thomas Ansell senior**, the father of Thomas Ansell junior, had offered 10 Guineas t Martha's Father as satisfaction, but he required 20 Guineas and might have taken 15. Since this offer was turned down, the father said that his son would have to take the consequences of the law.

Editorial comment;   Thomas Ansell senior was a man of some standing in the town.   In 1780, he was running a stage wagon and six horses to London and back, in partnership with a Mr. Mitchell, and in 1783, soon after this incident, he became the miller of the Smock Mill in Compton's Lane, on Horsham Common.   In his final will made shortly before he died, he was described as a farmer (HM MSS Cat. No. 2323, dated 11 September 1811).   He left his younger sons (Thomas and Charles) and his daughter Martha £200 each, while most of the remaining estate went to his eldest son, William.

Couple talking - Thomas Bewick *(design for pottery plate)*

Horsham Museum MSS Cat. No. 505, *extracted by* **Norrman Hewell**

The Queen vs George Langley for rape of Sarah Floate

Spring Assizes at Lewes – 16th March 1840

Case for the defence of the prisoner George Langley

The prisoner, George Langley, is a very respectable young man and has to date maintained an unimpeachable character for honesty, sobriety and industry, never having had a charge of any description brought against him, until this infamous one was trumped up by the prosecutrix, **Sarah Floate**, who is a girl of notorious bad character, for the purpose of extorting money from him, in which she was encouraged by **Hack**, the policeman. Had they succeeded, there was no doubt that they would have shared the spoil between them, as appears evident from his conduct after he had arrested the prisoner. Instead of advising the prisoner to produce evidence which would have cleared him, before the magistrates, he persuaded him not to call **Osborn**, the young man who was with him when he met the prosecutrix, and was only about 220 yards away from the spot where the alleged crime is stated to have been committed.

The morning after the occurrence, the prosecutrix, who has been living at home with her mother and father (a farm labourer) applied to Hack, the policeman. In consequence of his advice, she went accompanied by a married sister to **Mr Gibson**, a magistrate of Storrington, who knew something of her character and has since told the solicitor who now acts for the prisoner, that he doubted her statement when he took her sworn evidence, but then thought that he would have the opportunity to examine her more closely when she was confronted with the prisoner. Unfortunately for the prisoner, Mr Gibson's sister died and he was obliged to leave home to attend her funeral. The prisoner was therefore taken to Worthing, before Messrs. **Boghurst** and **Sanctuary**, who were unacquainted with the character of the prosecutrix. The prisoner, relying on his innocence and believing that the magistrates would dismiss the charge on hearing his statement of the circumstances, had no solicitor to attend for him and cross examine the prosecutrix. Consequently, he was committed to Lewes Gaol to take his trail on the capital charge, but was afterwards released on bail – two sureties of £100 each.

Two men in a cart, W.H. Pyne *(Etchings of Rustic Figures)*

It would appear that Hack, the policeman, was of a devious nature. He arrested the prisoner at about 4 o'clock on 20th October in the afternoon and took him to the Frankland Arms at Washington, near to where Mr Gibson lived, as it was expected that Mr Gibson and some other magistrates would meet there on the following morning. Between 8 and 9 on that morning, Hack received a message to take the prisoner to Worthing. Hack took no action until he was told this, when he gave instructions for a cart to follow them. They set out on foot between 11 and 12, and he told the prisoner that he had misread his instructions and that they were due in Worthing at 12. He hurried the prisoner with as much haste and secrecy as possible so that Langley's brother-in-law, **Wheatland**, and the witness Osborn should not be aware that the hearing was in Worthing. Wheatland and Osborn were at work in the stone quarry at Washington, but the postman saw Hack and the prisoner leaving for Worthing and informed them. They immediately left work and followed as fast as they could. Before they caught up, Hack had said several things to the prisoner – *"If you are acquitted I shall not have anything to bear your expenses, I shall have to pay them myself but if you get committed the county will pay them! I would not stand in your shoes for £2."* After the other two had caught up, Wheatland said to Osborn that he should go and speak the truth, whereupon Hack said *"I should advise you not to let that young lad* (meaning Osborn) *come forward and say anything as it may make the case worse and he may get punished for it."* Wheatland then said *"What harm can it do? I would speak the truth before the greatest magistrates in the world."* Shortly afterwards, the cart arrived and took Hack and the prisoner, leaving Wheatland and Osborn to walk. They could hardly get there before Langley was committed.

The prisoner was induced by what Hack said not to call Osborn before the magistrates. Hack is always employed to take the prisoners to gaol and his conduct in this instance warrants the conclusion that his advice to the prisoner not to call Osborn was given, not only to prevent the charge being dismissed, but to get the prisoner committed, upon which his fees were considerable. By a regulation made at the last Michaelmas Session, expenses are paid immediately after the delivery of the prisoners into the gaoler's custody, instead, as formerly, of waiting until after the following Assizes or Quarter Sessions. This was a temptation, which Hack had not sufficient honesty to withstand. Old **Floate**, the father of the prosecutrix, has stated in the presence of **Mr Henry Agate** and his servant **Scutt,** both witnesses, that his daughter would not have gone forward with the charge against Langley, had it not been for Hack. About a year ago, Hack endeavoured to persuade another young girl living in Washington parish, named **Ann Longhurst**, to swear a rape against **George Haines**, a young farmer in the neighbourhood, although he had never had intercourse with the girl. This could be substantiated by Longhurst, if it was thought that Hack would be examined, but it is evident that he cannot be called on to give any evidence.

The female part of the Floate family have a bad reputation. The prosecutrix and her unmarried sisters were kept at home, instead of going out to service, and were always running about together to clubs, fairs etc., where there was a chance of meeting with men, having sex and making money out of them. This might be proved by a waggon load of witnesses, if it were not for the expense of taking them to the Assizes. Recently, at Ashington, a married sister and her husband laid a trap for an old gentleman, who was in the habit of visiting the woman. While he was courting her, the husband who had concealed himself, came forward and they extorted about £6 from him under a threat of exposing and taking other measures against him. But true to type, they could not help boasting of their success, which brought them into such disrepute that the man lost his job and they were shunned by almost everybody and consequently were afterwards very much distressed.

The above evidence was felt necessary to show that the prisoner should not have been committed and that the charge would have been dismissed had it not been for the treacherous advice of the policeman Hack. The prisoner is a labourer and has no pecuniary resources, except those which he can obtain by his own industry, which are barely sufficient to maintain himself and his mother, who is about 70 years old and has been a widow for about 12 years, and has been chiefly supported by her son for the last four years, very much to his honour and credit. The consequences of this prosecution are to him and also his mother and family most serious and ruinous, due to the expenses he was put to after his committal, in procuring bail and in bringing so many witnesses 25 or 26 miles to Lewes.

The prisoner was at the time employed digging stone in a quarry at Washington for **Mr Goring** of Wiston. He worked there with his brother in law, Wheatland, and the witness Osborn. He was acquainted with the prosecutrix because he and Osborn and the prosecutrix were employed at Barns Farm *(in Storrington)* by Mr Henry Agate, working in the same field at the last harvest. On the day of the alleged rape, Tuesday 22nd October, the prisoner and Osborn (Wheatland having stayed at home that day, digging potatoes) left work and were returning home when they met the prosecutrix at about 5 pm. Osborn, who was walking ahead of the prisoner and had known the prosecutrix for some time, asked her how **Ian**

Charman was (Osborn had understood that he was courting her) and she replied that she did not know him. He then walked on, leaving the prisoner and the prosecutrix talking together. Osborn sat on the base of an ash tree about 155 yards further on, to wait for the prisoner, Langley, who did not come along until about half an hour later. After Osborn had been waiting about five minutes, the witness **Whitington** came along the road from Warminghurst, stopped to chat to him for about five minutes, and then went on his way towards Heath Common.   Whitington then went past the spot where the alleged transaction took place.   He heard someone talking and looked up and saw the prisoner talking to a woman he did not know. They were standing about 8 feet apart talking apparently very friendly together, but on seeing Whitington looking at her she went to a nearby gate, laid her head over it and pretended to cry or sob. Whitington on hearing that the prisoner had been sent to prison, expressed surprise to the person with whom he lodged, and they in turn informed Whitington's master, **Mr Walder.**

Passing by a gate - W.H. Pyne *(Etchings of Rustic Figures)*

About ten or fifteen minutes after Whitington had passed, **Richard Goatcher**, a thatcher who had been at work for Mr Golds of Warminghurst, came through a gate with his son, passed by Osborn and headed towards Heath Common. He overtook a female, who he did not see at first, because of the load he was carrying (He almost always has a basket on his shoulders when he goes to or returns from work and normally looks on the ground). On catching up with her, he noticed a piece of bramble bush across her gown tail and from her height (she and her sisters being very tall) he judged her to be the prosecutrix. As he passed, he noticed a sniffling or snubbing but as she held her handkerchief or shawl up he could not see her face. Nor did he see her face while they were walking together. He asked her if anything was the matter and gradually got out of her that she was upset back at the gate by a man who went rock digging at Washington named Mr Langley. Several times she repeated that he should pay for it! She also said she did not know the other young man who was with Langley, but he was very civil to her.

Some time after the prisoner had been committed, Mr Gibson sent for Goatcher and during his examination it was explained that snubbing meant pretending to cry. On 5th November, Hack came to Goatcher and was pumping him as to the evidence he could give regarding torn clothes. Goatcher said that the torn clothes report was false as they were not torn when he saw her, but Hack said it referred to the gathers of her petticoat and the shoulder straps of her stays.

Statement made to the magistrates by the prisoner, **George Langley**, to the best of his recollection.

On meeting the prosecutrix, the prisoner shook hands with her and enquired after her health, then asked if she would let him walk home with her. She said that she was expecting a visitor as far as she knew. He said that he would like a private word with her and they walked down the road together, holding hands. He said that he would very much like to spend the night with her and she said that she was too near to marriage for that. He offered half a crown or a present to that value, she said she hardly had time and they walked on hand in hand to the gateway, entrance to a field. While they were having intercourse against the gate, Langley saw someone coming along from Warminghurst whom he thought was a boy. It was in fact, Whitington. Langley said that it was a little too public and they did not need to expose themselves to everyone, but should go into the field. He opened the gate and pulled off his frock, which was tied round his shoulders by the sleeves, and spread it on the ground. He took the prosecutrix by the hands, laid her down and completed the act. While the prisoner was pulling up his trousers, he looked over the gate towards Warminghurst and saw a person approaching. This was Goatcher, and he told the prosecutrix that he was coming. He suggested that it might be the person she expected and that she might have been seen, because of her light bonnet, while his clothes were dark. She had better go out to meet him and if it was not the person that she was expecting, he would go and join her. He heard her say to Goatcher *"against the gate"*, and then he went to join Osborn and they went home together.

The case for the defence

From the prisoner's account of what took place before the magistrates, it would appear that had the prosecutrix been compelled to give her own evidence unassisted by her mother, and not encouraged by the magistrates, there would not have been anything like a *prima facie* case to warrant a committal. The magistrates put leading questions which drew forth corresponding answers, and when she and her mother hesitated, suggested such answers as made a case on which, there being no one on the prisoner's behalf to shake it by cross examination, they committed him. The following is a sample of the whole proceeding.

The prisoner stated that the prosecutrix could not recollect on which day it took place, although it was only four days after the occurrence. First she said it was on Thursday, then on Wednesday and afterwards on being prompted by her mother she stated Tuesday. She said that she did no know the prisoner or the young man who was with him, but Goatcher stated that she said that she knew the prisoner but did not know the young man, though Osborn has known her and she him for a considerable time and they had frequently met each other. They, as well as Langley, had worked in the same field for a week during the last harvest. The prosecutrix was asked by Mr Sanctuary, one of the examining magistrates, in what way the prisoner confined her hands, did he kneel upon your chest? She answered in the affirmative. Mrs Floate, the mother, was asked if there was any blood on her chemise, the question implying that the magistrate thought that she was a virgin, or that she had received some serious injury, and mother replied *"Yes, a little"*. Upon being asked where the chemise was, she hesitated and did not answer, but Mr Boghurst the committing magistrate rendered one unnecessary by saying *"I suppose you washed it"*. The prosecutrix was cunning enough to say that she did not make a noise because she would have been heard by Osborn, Whitington, Goatcher or his boy, or at any rate one of them, and if she had made any resistance, it must have been seen by Osborn who was not that far away and had an unobstructed view. She said that she was so low and her feelings so much hurt that she could make no resistance. Her appearance and character will give a lie to that.

There was one circumstance which struck the prisoner's solicitor very forcibly as making it impossible for a man, even of gigantic strength, forcing a female - if she made the least resistance - through the gateway, if the gate opened towards the road. Consequently, he went and examined the spot. He found that all the gates along that road opened towards the road. He went into great detail to prove that it would be impossible for a man to force an unwilling woman through such a gateway. He also noted that there was no hard footing there and, due to the rains and the turning of cattle there to graze on the side of the road, it was much churned up. If the prisoner had forced the prosecutrix through the gateway then she would have been covered in mud, which must have been seen by Goatcher, who stated that her clothes were not even disordered. Instead of being forced, she must have had time to pick her way through to avoid the dirt. Upon putting the above evidence to the magistrates, Mr Sanctuary stated that the prosecutrix had said that the prisoner had lifted the gate up with his foot and pushed it open, which he could not possibly have done because the gate opened towards him. On referring to **Mr Tribe**, the magistrates clerk, no such statement could be found. This shows that the prisoner did not receive fair treatment before the magistrates.

Evidence will be given by **Charles Osborn**, **John Whitington** and **Richard Goatcher** as to what they witnessed, as above, and other witnesses will give evidence to support the prisoner's case.

George Brading has stated that he had had intercourse with the prosecutrix on several occasions. After the East Chiltington Club Meeting (which is the first Thursday in June) he left with her about 10 pm and remained with her till 2 am, during which time they had intercourse. On Saturday after last Michaelmas, the day of Steyning Fair he had intercourse with her on Washington Common. She is a constant attendant of fairs, clubs etc.

John Scutt, who has been married about seventeen years and lives at his master's house at Barns Farm. His master is Mr Henry Agate. For about eleven years he has frequently seen Sarah Floate romping with the men on the farm, when she was a distance from the house and out of Mr Agate's sight. He has sometimes seen **William Moulding** kiss and maul her about and even throw her to the ground. He has also seen her in the company of another young girl, the daughter of a **Mrs Wells**, come to the farm and hold up her handkerchief as a signal for **Edmund Parker**, who lived with Mr Agate, to follow her, but as soon as Parker saw who it was, he would have nothing to do with them. He has seen her frequently conduct herself in such a manner as no prudent girl would and as he would be sorry to see and would not allow a daughter of his. He has also received instructions from Mr Agate to inform her father that if she did not conduct herself better, they would both lose their jobs.

Mr Henry Agate has occupied a considerable farm called Barns Farm for several years and has employed the father and family of the prosecutrix including Sarah Floate herself. Their work has been varied, including the following jobs: stone picking, weeding, haying and harvesting. Mr Agate had found her generally taking every opportunity of romping and gossiping with the men and has on one or two occasions found her in very suspicious situations with men, so much so that he directed John Scutt to warn her father that if this conduct continued, he would not employ them.   Mr Agate can also confirm the general character and habit of the prosecutrix of running about to fairs and clubs and to the general good character of the prisoner since he has known him.

Mr Henry Hills, the relieving officer of the union, reported that on the first Sunday in October, having been to put the quarterly meeting notice on the door of Warminghurst Church, was returning home to Washington in the middle of the afternoon when he saw the prosecutrix and a man in a hovel near the roadside on Heath Common, where they had evidently been having intercourse as the man was pulling up his breeches. As soon as they saw Mr Hills, the man ran into the field and the prosecutrix came out past the witness.   Mr Hills can also confirm the general character of Sarah Floate and the good character of George Langley.

Mr Henry Floate has occupied a farm in Washington Parish for some years and has known the prosecutrix' family. He confirms that Sarah and her sisters have remained at home, instead of going out to service, and have run about to fairs and clubs and he has latterly known the prisoner who has conducted himself very steadily and properly.

Mr John Kaye and **Mr Thomas Baines** (one of the prisoner's Bail) will both speak to prove the good character of the prisoner.

Stone diggers - W.H. Pyne *(Microcosm)*

Horsham Museum MSS Cat. No. 307, *extracted by* **Audrey Goffe**

The King against William Evans, for riot in a Methodist meeting

Sussex, Christmas Sessions, 18 Geo. 3ʳᵈ (1777)

The indictment stated that *"the Defendant on 9ᵗʰ November 18ᵗʰ, 1777, at Horsham did willingly and of purpose maliciously and contemptuously go into a certain congregation permitted and allowed by Law ... and recorded at the General Quarter Sessions of the Peace for the said County, caused disquiet and disturbed the same congregation to the Evil Example and against the peace."* The statute referred to was one of 1688 (1 William & Mary) . entitled, *"An Act for exempting their Majesties Protestant subjects dissenting ... from the Church of England from the penalties of Certain Laws".* [Its provisions were set out in detail.]

The case for the prosecution.

At the Quarter Sessions held for the Western part of Sussex at Midhurst on 8ᵗʰ January 1776, **Mr. Thomas Mann** *(a Methodist)* and other inhabitants of Horsham claimed that for a place set aside for divine worship, according to the above mentioned Act of Parliament, a certificate had been registered at Sessions held at Horsham, and the said Mr. Mann was in consequence granted a licence to teach and preach therein.

It was said that *"the Defendant and others of the same profligate stamp had frequently made it their business when the congregation had assembled to perform their devotions, to go to the place of worship and cause a disturbance by laughing, talking and swearing, disquieting the congregation and preventing the performance of religious duties. Mr. Mann for a considerable time took no notice of the behaviour other than reproving those involved and exhorting them to quit the Meeting if they could not act with propriety. Finding this had no effect, and the Defendant was obviously the ring leader and more daring and insolent than the rest, Mr. Mann laid information of the fact before a Magistrate upon which a warrant was signed under the Statute of 1 Wm. and Mary, and Evans was apprehended. Not being able to find a Surety, his committal was proposed. Evans thought it best to relent and asked forgiveness of Mr. Mann and the Magistrate and made a solemn promise not to offend again and confirmed by a number of profane wishes and imprecations to himself in case of breach of them, solicited the Magistrate to forego the committal. Evans was discharged".*

Claims by the prosecution included:-

• That Evans had several times before the 9ᵗʰ November last disturbed the congregation.

• That the defendant came into the meeting on Sunday, 9ᵗʰ November and by laughing, talking and swearing had disquieted and disturbed the congregation.

• That the defendant had called at the house of **Charles Gilburd** in the night of 9ᵗʰ November to collect his coat, saying he had been guilty of a RIOT at the Methodist Meeting and he must go off.

Editorial comment:: There are some entries in John Baker's diary of relevance to this case.

7 February 1776   Charles last night went to hear one Woodgate, a Methodist from London, preach at a sort of barn, near Mr. Dawson's. *(This may have been at Coote's Farm on Horsham Common since this is shown as having been occupied by George Dawson, son of Mr. Dawson, in the Tithe Map schedule of 1840. There was also mention of houses owned by the Dawson family on Horsham Common in wills made by his brother, John Dawson - HM MSS Cat. Nos. 2345 and 2348).* It seems when Tasker the tallow-chandler died three or four years ago, one Mann from Petworth came and took the house and trade and introduced Methodism, and made some converts preaching at his own house. *(It seems likely that this house was on the south-east corner of Market Square, where no. 7 The Causeway now is).* But now they have a licence from the Sessions to preach at this house and began last night. They have hymns too sung. Young Sowton (was) asked to act as clerk...Sowton was one of the top hands among our singers *(presumably at the Parish Church)*; he and his wife and mother, John Pavey and wife and others are made Methodists.

21 April 1776   (All the Blunt party came and) went to hear the Methodist Preacher on the Common.

6 September 1776   Mrs. Martin told me of a *fracas* between Mr. Flint (i.e. Fleet) and Mann, the Methodist preacher, and others, last Sunday night, at Methodists' meeting, and their going to Sir Charles Eversfield and others for a warrant. Mr. Fleet went away to London about 11 last Monday, having lodged here the night before. Our Charles Lewis was with him at the Methodists' meeting on Sunday evening when the thing happened.

3 November 1776   Charles told me that he and Ann *(went)* to Methodist meeting ..où *(where)* Mr. Brown catechising children and all his sermon about Zaccheus (whom he called Yaccheus) climbing the trees - excellent singing and many women's voices, he said.

(These extracts are taken from the extracts from John Baker's diary, edited by Wilfred Scawen Blunt, which were published in the Sussex Archaeological Collections, Vol. LII, *pp. 38-81, and* The Diary of John Baker, *edited by Philip C. Yorke, published by Hutchinson and Co. in 1931. It is often necessary to check both sources to get the full story, as both editors make omissions).*

John Wesley (1703-1791), one of the founders of the Methodist Church, preaching

The King (on the Prosecution of John Hamblin) against Francis Sergison, gent. and others (John Kimber and John Marchant) (for Riot).

To be tried at East Grinstead Assizes on Tuesday, 27th March 1787

The Indictment states that Defendants on 2nd September in 26th year of the reign of present Majesty (Geo. III) *"with force and arms at the Parish of Cuckfield did unlawfully, riotously, tumultuously, violently and outrageously make a great noise Disturbance and Affray near and about the Dwellinghouse of the Prosecutor there situate did unlawfully riotously and tumultuously stay and continue near to and about said dwellinghouse making such their noise Disturbance and Affray for a long space of time (to wit) for 2 hours and during that time did riotously shoot off and discharge a certain gun loaded with gunpowder and leaden shot against the said dwellinghouse and there not only greatly terrified and Alarm'd the Prosecutor and his family and disturbed and disquieted them in the Peaceable and quiet possession use and occupation of the said dwellinghouse but also broke to pieces shattered and damaged the glass (to wit) 20 panes of glass of large value there affixed and belonging to the said windows and therewith loud and horrid Oaths and Improcations Unlawfully riotously, and tumultuously menaced and threatened the Prosecutor to shoot him through the Body and other Wrongs then and there did to the Prosecutor To his great Damage and against the Peace".* The defendants pleaded not guilty.

The case for the defence

The defendant, **Mr. Francis Sergison**, is the second and youngest son of **Francis Sergison, Esq.,** of Cuckfield Place, *"a Man of Family and Fortune"* and the late High Sheriff of the County. **John Kimber** is his park keeper and gamekeeper and the other defendant, **John Marchant**, is one of his postillions and a helper in the stables. The prosecutor, **John Hamblin**, is by profession a turner, and the witness **James Thorpe** a day labourer, but their real character amongst their acquaintances and the neighbourhood in general is that of common poachers. For several years they have supported themselves by their industry and dexterity in killing and taking the game. Hamblin keeps a black and white wire haired spaniel which is reputed an excellent dog of its kind. He and Thorpe have been frequently seen by neighbouring farmers about their grounds and complaints have been made at Cuckfield Place, in order they might be watched and detected in their practice of poaching and prevented from treading down, spoiling and injuring the corn, etc. In consequence of these complaints, and from their notorious character, the defendant Kimber had been out many nights, watching for them, and had often seen Hamblin's dog about the grounds, but the owner and his companion Thorpe had always had the good luck to escape his vigilance.

(In late August 1786, Kimber had good reason to suspect that Hamblin and Thorpe had been out poaching, and reported his suspicions at Cuckfield Park, at which point Francis Sergison determined to go out himself to watch with Kimber).

About 11 o'clock on the evening of Saturday 2nd September, the day on which the riot is laid by the indictment to have been committed, the defendants went from Cuckfield Place with the intent of watching Hamblin and Thorpe out of their houses and following and detecting them in their old business of poaching. Mr. Sergison and Kimber took guns for the purpose of shooting the prosecutor's dog should they see him hunting after game. When they came to Ansty Turnpike Gate, Mr. Sergison went into Heaseman's house to enquire if he had seen anything of Thorpe or Hamblin. Kimber and Marchant waited near the gate till his return. Mr. Sergison gave Kimber his gun, who stayed behind, whilst Mr. Sergison and Marchant walked along the road by Thorpe's and Hamblin's houses. They saw lights in the chamber *(bedroom)* windows of both houses and then returned back to Kimber. It is thought that Hamblin or his wife were at this time upon the look-out and saw them pass and knew they were there. The three defendants then went over into the fields on the east side of the road and crept along under the hedge adjoining the road until they came opposite the two cottages (which stand on the west side of the road) and then laid down under the hedge. In a short time Hamblin came out of his house and whistled to his dog for some time and then went into his shop. After working there for a few minutes he came out and hallood out in a kind of laughing manner, *"Damme Thorpe, Damme Thorpe, there is somebody going to rob the house".* He then clapped his hands and encouraged the dog who came twice at the hedge where Mr. Sergison lay, very near his face. Hamblin came to the hedge and struck violently at the place and said, *"Damme, I'll see who you are"* upon which Mr. Sergison jumped up and over into the road and said, *"I'll let you know who I am, what Business had you to strike at me"*. Hamblin replied, *"I ask pardon Sir, I did not know who it was."* Mr. Sergison said, *"Have you a mind to strike me now?"* Hamblin said, *"No Sir."* Mr. Sergison then said, *"I'll not strike you"*, but added *"You and Thorpe were going out to night poaching or at your old tricks. Whose Dog is that you set at me? What business had you to set the Dog at me."* Hamblin said, *"It is my Dog. I keep it for a House Dog."* Mr. Sergison said to Kimber, *"Shoot the Dog Kimber. Why don't you shoot the Dog?"* Kimber replied he would as soon as he could and getting sight of the Dog he shot at him in the direction of full South. The dog cried out and ran into the Hamblin house. Kimber offered several times to go into the house and fetch the dog out and kill him before Mr. Sergison's face, if he would say the word. Mr. Sergison replied, *"No, no. I'll not have you go into the house after him by any means at such an Improper Time of Night, for if you have a Right to take him out to Night, you have the same Right to Morrow Morning."* Mr. Sergison then said to Hamblin, *"Where was you last Monday night, you was not at home?"* Hamblin hesitated. Mr. Sergison said, *"You and Thorpe were out poaching".* Mr. Sergison then asked Hamblin whether Thorpe was in his house. Hamlin replied he was not as he was in bed and asleep. Mr. Sergison then went to Thorpe's house and called out, *"Thorpe, Thorpe."* His wife looked out of the window and said her husband was in bed and asleep. Thorpe then came and looked out of the window. Mr. Sergison said, *"Are you Thorpe?"* *"Yes, yes, I am."* Mr. Sergison returned, *"You certainly are Thorpe. Then you may go to bed again and I am sure you are at home".* Thorpe said, *"I have been ill for some time and have not been out."* Mr. Sergison said to Kimber, *"Come along, we'll not be disappointed,. We'll go our Rounds."* They walked down the road a small distance and returned to the turnpike house *(Ansty tollgate)*, where they all went in, and having stayed a little while returned to Cuckfield Place, about half past 12 o'clock.

Two men with a stick and a dog - W.H. Pyne *(Etchings of Rustic Figures)*

The defendants claimed that they heard no glass break after the gun was fired at the dog nor was any complaint then made or afterwards at Cuckfield Place of its having been done, or to any neighbouring magistrate, nor did the family ever entertain the most remote idea or apprehension of any prosecution being commenced or of hearing again of the affair, of which the above is an exact account, and it is evident from the testimony after stated, that the Prosecutor (Hamblin) himself never had any intention of the kind. He has been persuaded and instigated thereto by a **Mr. Bryant**, an Attorney at Reigate, and the **Rev. Mr. Thomas Evans**, now of Seaford, but formerly Curate of Cuckfield. The Rev. Mr. Evans, whilst curate of Cuckfield for several years, received the greatest friendship and civilities from the Sergison family, living almost entirely at the house and being assisted frequently in pecuniary matters by them. But being disappointed in his expectations of the living of Slaugham, which they thought fit to give to another gentleman, he afterwards behaved in the most insolent and ungrateful manner. One day having given Mr. Sergison the lie on the road near Cuckfield he, *"from natural warmth of Temper and being bred in the Army"*, could not refrain striking Evans. This was the subject of an action in which Bryant was concerned as attorney for Evans.

On the 2nd and 3rd October last they came with 2 other persons, one of whom was Bryant's black servant, to shooting on the manor and lands of Mr. Sergison just by his house, on purpose to insult him, on which occasion both the young Mr. Sergisons went out to prevent their shooting, and having demanded their licences, an altercation took place between **Mr. Warden Sergison** (Mr.Sergison's eldest son) and the said Bryant during which Bryant addressed himself to the defendant Sergison, *"G- d- me young Fellow, as to you I'll have your hand at the Bar upon the Black Act, if I don't G- d- me"* and Evans at the same time said he had seen the broken windows of the prosecutor Hamblin, and in a few days put his own collar on the Hamblin's dog. It must come out upon cross examination of the prosecutor and Thorpe that they have been frequently since that period examined by Bryant. They were sent for to the *Kings Head*, Cuckfield, at the beginning of January last, and persuaded to go to Lewes to prefer an indictment against the defendants. Bryant and Evans have promised to support Hamblin at their own expense. Bryant has indeed avowed the part he takes therein, having been heard to declare at Lewes Sessions that it was *"a BRAT of his own, and he would take care to nurse it properly"*. If it be possible in the course of the trial to fix it equally upon Evans, Mr. Francis Sergison (senior) is determined to bring an action against him for a conspiracy against his sons, after the acquittal of the defendants, which there can be but very little doubt of their obtaining in a case like the present. The defence is to be based on precedents to show that *"the assembly was a lawful one and without any evil intent"* and that *"the Indictment states the gun was shot at the windows and the Defendants threatened to shoot the Prosecutor through the Body"*. The fact is that the gun was discharged at the prosecutor's dog and in a direction north and south and the house was at least [blank] yards to the west. If any windows were broken (which seems impossible) it must have happened from the shot recoiling from the ground. The motive for shooting the dog was from the defendants' knowledge of his being used by the prosecutor and Thorpe for the purpose of destroying game. Kimber, who fired the shot, was and is gamekeeper under Mr. Sergison for the Manor of Cuckfield in which the affair happened. If the defendant Sergison did wrong in commanding Kimber to shoot and wound the prosecutor's dog, it should be the subject of a civil action and not an indictment for riot.

Editorial comment:. This case concerns the Sergison family of Cuckfield Park, who were somewhat eccentric, to say the least. The rather odd behaviour of Francis Sergison, the chief defendant in this case, is perhaps less surprising if one recalls something of his family background, and subsequent history. Ann, the mother of Francis Sergison, was the only child of Michael Warden, who inherited Cuckfield Place; but her right to succeed to the estates was disputed in a Chancery case in which it was claimed that she was not born in wedlock, and that her mother, Sarah Dean, had been a servant. Ann claimed that her parents had contracted a previous secret marriage in the Fleet Prison, and although she was never able to produce any evidence to support this claim, her right to inherit was confirmed. In 1784, Ann became Lady of the Manor and Dame of Cuckfield Place and her husband, Francis Jefferson, took the name Sergison and became an active "Squire" of Cuckfield. After his death in 1793, she married a much younger man, the Rev. Thomas Scutt, in 1804, but the marriage ended within a year in a deed of separation, under which Dame Ann allowed her husband £1,000 a year. At the time of her death in 1806, she had an income of £8,000 a year in rents, and was able to support her two spendthrift sons, Warden and Francis Sergison, and save for herself a private fortune of £17,000. Her will, dated 27 October 1806, left all her property in trust, with the interest on her capital divided between her two sons for their joint lives; to the survivor during his life and, after their decease, to transfer the estate in trust to any of their surviving children. The will made no mention of her daughter Ann, wife of the Rev. William Pritchard, from whom she was estranged, though her children were mentioned in the entail. It was stipulated that her private fortune should go to her sons' children (if any).

Warden Sergison, *who was a prominent member of the Prince Regent's circle in Brighton, lost his wife and had no children; he died at the age of forty-five in 1811, having fought an unsuccessful campaign to be elected as one of the Sussex M.P.s in 1807. He petitioned against the result in 1808, with Thomas Charles Medwin as his chief agent, but the costs of this action were ruinous, and the result was not overturned. His brother, Francis Sergison, had by now proved himself to be even more arrogant and high-handed than he was as a young man in this case, and was generally regarded as a wild and disreputable character. His mother had bought him promotion in the army, and he was Lt. Col. of the 62nd Regiment when he was committed to the Sheriff's Prison in Dublin for debt in 1806. He had with him a woman whom he said was his wife, but she died there. Two weeks later he married a woman he met in the prison,* Elizabeth Ann Cronin, *after an acquaintanceship of ten days. She was the widow of a coach-builder, and had a son by Lord Ely in 1804, and another by a Mr. Fitzgerald in 1805. Francis was most anxious to have an heir in the hope that the child would inherit his mother's private fortune. He was very angry when Elizabeth Ann did not become pregnant and she told a friend,* Mrs. Gibson, *that* "she dreaded the Colonel would have her life if she was not with child". *She conspired with Mrs. Gibson and others to obtain a new-born baby and pass it off as her own, which she did successfully. The family left Ireland in 1807 and the baby was baptised at St. Ann's Westminster on 8 January 1808 as* Elizabeth Ann Harriet Sergison.

After his brother's death in 1811, Francis - coming in great haste to take possession of his estates - was said to have stopped at the top of the hill from Handcross leading down to Staplefield, and shouted "It's all mine, all mine!" *But he died within the year, in 1812. His widow continued to live at Cuckfield Place until her supposed daughter was thirteen, by which time Francis' sister, Ann Pritchard, had been approached by people in Dublin offering information about the true parentage of Harriet. This led to a long and costly lawsuit, which opened on 11 July 1820 and concluded in December with the jury finding* "the young lady illegitimate" *and allowing Ann Pritchard to inherit the Cuckfield estate, now the richest in Sussex, and change her name to Sergison. After* Ann Pritchard Sergison *became the Lady of the Manor at Cuckfield in 1820, at the age of 57, she came to be known as* 'the wicked Dame Sergison' *on account of* "her vile and vindictive temper...hot and spiteful". *She started to pay off olds scores against people who had offended her in the past, and there are many stories of her misdeeds. After she died in 1848, at the age of 85, a local clergyman said that he thought she must have been insane. She soon became the subject of ghost stories at the gate of Cuckfield Park as country people said that she was too wicked to rest in her grave. Finally three clergymen were said to have held a service of exorcism at the church and her ghost was said to have stopped haunting the highway..*

(These notes are based on Maisie Wright's book, A Chronicle of Cuckfield, *revised edition, 1991, which devotes a chapter to the Sergison family)*

Cuckfield Place (from *The Brighton Road*)

Horsham Museum MSS Cat. No. 328, *extracted by* **Norman Hewell**

Slanderous Language to a respectable Attorney - request for Counsel's Opinion on whether to bring a case

Saturday 19th February 1785 was Market Day. At an inn on that day, in a Market Town, in the presence of about a dozen persons there was a case of character defamation. **Mr A.B.** an attorney of respectable connections and reputable practice and character was insulted by **Mr J.,** a schoolmaster, who had been involved in a recent case in which Mr A.B. had judged to the satisfaction of everyone present, and in all fairness and perfect character. The following is a list of expressions said to have been used and some of them were used more than once.

You are a Petty Fogger! (Pettifog – to act in petty cases)   You are nothing but a Petty Fogger!
You are a Petty Fogging Attorney who ruined the W......... family!
Keep your head out of the pillory! (Innuendo that Mr A.B. had perjured himself in a case between the brothers W…)
You have cheated all the country, you cheat everyone you can lay hold of!
I believe that you have very little business, no one will employ you!
You do all the dirty work, you are a paltry fellow and would have run away years ago, if it had not been for your father!
You are kept by the parish, your father won't trust you with a pound of sugar!

Although Mr A.B.'s reputation is too well established to suffer any injury or damage by the above abuse, he is determined, if possible, to punish Mr J. for his insolent conduct and he understands that all or many of the words spoken by Mr J. to him, as a professional man, are actionable and that therefore it will only be necessary to prove those words to entitle himself to a verdict. Mr A.B. quotes the following words from similar cases, which have been previously adjudged actionable: -

He is a Champorter!
He has no more law than Mr C. a bull!
He will milk her purse and fill his own large pockets!
Thou canst not read!
Thou art a cozening knave and gettest thy living by extortion and didst cozen one pidgeon in a bill of costs of £10!
He is a paltry fellow, his credit doth begin to crack, he doth deal on both sides!
Have you brought home the £40 you stole!
He is a dunce and will get little by the law!

Your opinion therefore requested, whether any or all and which of the words spoken by Mr J. to Mr A.B. are actionable, and are desired to point out such as will be most essential to be successful.

Counsel's Opinion

The words above stated to have been spoken of Mr A.B. being spoken of him in his presence are actionable. I think all expressions are actionable, therefore it is needless to strike out any.

W. Baldwin, 1st March 1785

Horsham Museum MSS Cat. No. 304, *extracted by* *Audrey Goffe*

The King against Edmund and Robert Drewitt, for theft from an Exciseman

Lent Assizes   1777

(Note on the document;   Brief to Mr. Lade. For the Prisoners)

Indictment for stealing a horse, 6 bags of tea and 4 cases, the property of Thomas Gray, of St. Andrews Holborn.

The case for the defence

Robert Drewitt, in or about August then last, had been employed as a servant by **Thomas Gray** (an Exciseman) to fetch him goods which the said Thomas Gray had purchased of smugglers in the country in order to convict them, from thence to the Excise Office in London.   During this employment a plan had been concocted by him, his brother **Edmund** and one **Henry Oldfield** and was brought about by the persuasion of Oldfield that Thomas Gray and Robert Drewitt should be attacked by the said Edmund Drewitt and Oldfield on an appointed evening at a certain spot and time, and be robbed of their horses and goods.   The plan was put into execution on a dark night in August at 10 o'clock.   The horses were turned loose and found the next day by Gray and Robert Drewitt, who had gone together in quest of the robbers.   The 6 bags of tea had been sold by Edmund and Robert Drewitt, so neither horses nor goods had been found upon them.

Soon after the robbery, Oldfield was committed to Horsham gaol for goose stealing (for which he was to be tried at the Assizes) and had since given information about the facts above and upon which Robert and Edmund Drewitt were apprehended.   Before this affair the prisoners were looked upon as honest men and would have many reputable persons speak of their good character.   They had been drawn into crime entirely by the said Oldfield – a most infamous character.   The Defendants depend upon that and strict cross examination of Oldfield for their only defence.

Editorial comment: In 1799, two brothers called Robert and William Drewitt, of Midhurst, were committed to Horsham Gaol on a charge of robbing the Mail coach at North Heath - possibly the same Robert Drewitt as in this case, or a relation. They were caught in an attempt to get cash for a bank draft of £55, part of their booty.   They were tried at the Spring Assizes at East Grinstead and sentenced to death.   While waiting for their execution in Horsham Gaol, there was a report that an attempt would be made to rescue them. A strong military guard was placed at the Gaol and they were brought out four or five hours before the usual time, as a precaution. Robert was much agitated but said nothing, but William harangued the crowd and protested his innocence.   After the executions, the bodies were taken back to Horsham Gaol to be put in irons and taken to the scene of the crime at North Heath, where they were gibbeted on gallows 32 feet high, amid scenes that resembled a fair.   The bodies hung there for three years, but it was the last time that criminals were gibbetted in Sussex. (Their story is told in full in William Albery's Millennium, *on pages 295-296).*

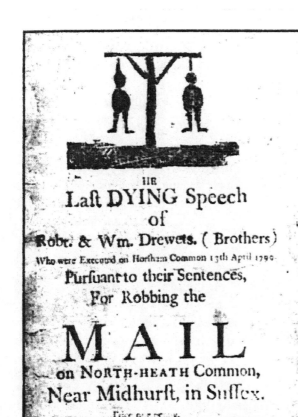

THE Last DYING Speech of Robt. & Wm. Drewets. (Brothers) Who were Executed on Horsham Common 13th April 1799. Pursuant to their Sentences, For Robbing the

MAIL

on NORTH-HEATH Common, Near Midhurst, in Suffex.

Robert and Wm. DREWETS, (Brothers) were born near Midhurst in Suffex, of Poor, but honeft parents; it being out of their power to give them but little education, having fo large a family.—Poor unhappy Men! they learnt nothing but Vice: William being the eldeft brother always took the lead in his wicked actions, but at length the hand of Juftice overtook him and put an end to his wicked actions.

He has left a Widow, and fix fmall children.

When young men begin to run aftray,
The law of God is by them done away.
Robert being the younger Brother and daily with William, give way to the advice of his Brother, by which he met with his unhappy end.

The hour arrived which was to put an end to the lives of thefe unhappy Criminals, they received the Sacrament, and after which they were placed in a cart and conducted to Horfham Common.

At the Gallows, Wm. declar'd his Innocence, and hop'd that the Spectators would take a warning, and not Hang People wrongfully.

Beware in youth, of their untimely fate,
And turn to God before it is too late
Be not induc'd to unlawful gain,
That was the caufe of their unhappy end,

Live honeft and juft, & you'll be, Rewarded to all eternity.

After hanging the ufual time, their Bodies were convey'd to the place where they committed the Robbery to be Hanged in CHAINS.

Broadsheet giving the last dying speech of William Drewitt (from Albery's *Millennium*)

Man leading horse with baskets containing bags - W.H. Pyne (*Etchings of Rustic Figures*)

The King vs John Stenning, James Stenning junior and William Stenning for theft from Rev'd Morgan Evans, Clerk, Curate of Kirdford and Wisborough Green.

Epiphany Quarter Sessions – 1785

For feloniously taking and carrying away from and out of the yard situate in the parish of Wisborough Green on 24th November last, two pear trees to the value of 5 shillings, the property of the **Rev. Morgan Evans,** Clerk.[9]

The three prisoners live in one house with their father **Pat Stenning**[10] and have repeatedly been indicted and tried for theft but so far they have had the good fortune to have escaped the hands of justice. This is to the anger and disappointment of the farmers and neighbours of Wisborough Green. They have no visible means of supporting themselves and are from that circumstance, as well as their notorious bad character, suspected of living by pilfering, thieving and committing depredations upon all those who have the misfortune to live near to them.

The Rev. Morgan Evans had been given two pear trees by **Mr John Haines**[11] and they were left in the yard at the rear of his house. He saw them on the Tuesday evening 23rd November, but on Thursday morning they were gone. He went into the yard between seven and eight in the morning and noticed that they were not there. Suspicion immediately fell on **John Stenning** who had been employed by **Mr Pavey,**[12] a local farmer, to deliver a load of stubble to the yard on the previous Tuesday, so that the trees could be planted.

The Rev. Evans obtained a search warrant from **Mr Smith** of Stopham and then on Monday 29th November accompanied by the constable, **Daniel Hurst, Mr Thomas Elliott,**[13] **Mr Richard Elms**[14] and others, went to the Stenning home and carried out a search of the premises. They found two pear trees, one of which had been sawn and shaped to be used as a gun stock and the other had had the end sawn off. John and William were at home at the time and John claimed that the trees had been given to him, six or seven years ago, by his landlord, the present Mr Symonds' father, who had died five or six years earlier. However, Mr. Evans was positive that the trees were those which he had lost. John and William Stenning were arrested and brought before Mr Smith who committed John to Horsham Gaol and William to Petworth House of Correction. **James Stenning**, the other brother, had made off just before the constable had arrived.[15] He was seen by Mr Pavey about half an hour after the others had left, getting out of a ditch and leaning over a hedge to talk to his wife. He was later arrested and taken to Petworth.

People in conversation - W.H. Pyne (*Etchings of Rustic Figures*)

---

9   Sussex Record Society, Vol. 82, *West Sussex Land Tax 1785,* Wisbrough Green, pp. 242-7. The Rev. Morgan Evans lived at a house called Hooks.

10   As above. Pat Stenning does not appear in the Land Tax records.

11   As above. Mr. John Hains owned Wildsbrood.

12   As above. There is no Mr. Pavey listed, but a Mr. Pacy owned Old House Farm and other properties.

13   As above. Mr. Thomas Elliott owned Loves and other properties.

14   As above. Richard Elmes lived at Three Lanes End.   He and Thomas Elliott were collectors of Land Tax.

15   As above.   James Steyning *(sic)* lived in a small cottage owned by Mr. Simmons *(sic)* in the Mens End area of Wisborough Green.

Note - **John Stenning also charged with theft from Mr Elliott of Wisborough Green, Yeoman**

John Stenning will also be indicted for stealing from out of the barn of Mr Elliott of Wisborough Green,[16] Yeoman, half a bushel of wheat on 15th August 1784.

Mr Elliott's thresher, **John Man**, on missing wheat from the hoop in the barn, on several occasions, reported the matter to his master. Mr Elliott then took two samples of wheat and sent them to two mills in the neighbourhood with instruction that if anyone brought in similar wheat for grinding, they were to let him know. A few days later, **Greenfield Stenning**, who rents the windmill, came to Mr Elliott and said that John Stenning's wife had brought a similar bushel of wheat which she said her husband had bought from **John Mitchell** of ?Wimblehurst.[17] Mr Elliott went to Stenning's wife and accused her husband of the theft. She said that it had come from Mr Mitchell, but a few days later, Mr Mitchell denied selling any wheat to John Stenning. John Stenning, being in custody for the former offence, told Mr Elliott that he had not purchased any wheat that year and that the wheat he had sent to the mill was leaved wheat.

This account given by the thresher, John Man, Mr Elliott and John Mitchell will be sufficient to call upon the prisoner to account for the way in which he obtained the wheat. The two samples of wheat will be produced and compared in court.

A summons was served upon John Mitchell, Farmer of Wisborough Green, and Greenfield Stenning, Miller of the same place, to attend the Quarter Sessions to be held at Midhurst on Monday in the week after Epiphany, Monday 10th January 1785 to determine divers felonies, trespasses and other ill deeds. Indictment to be tried between us and John Stenning for a felony on our behalf. 7th October 1784

Passing the word - W.H. Pyne (*Etchings of Rustic Figures*)

---

[16]   Sussex Record Society, Vol. 82, *West Sussex Land Tax 1785,* Wisbrough Green, pp. 242-7.. This is presumably Thomas Elliott of Loves, mentioned previously.

[17]   As above. John Mitchell lived at a farm called Amblehurst, not Wimblehurst.

Horsham Museum MSS Cat. No. 375, *extracted by* **John Hurd**

The King (on prosecution of John Botting) against Edward Bailey

Epiphany Sessions at Chichester 1796

Indictment for feloniously stealing 19 fowls at Washington on 28 November.

Endorsed: *guilty Botany Bay 7 years*

Case for the prosecution

On Sunday morning 29th November **Elizabeth Botting**, wife of **John Botting** of Washington, was missing 19 fowls - the neighbours had heard nothing. On the following Tuesday **John Cuckney** a higler[18] of Steyning, came for butter; as he had frequently bought fowls from her she mentioned the loss of her fowls. Cuckney said that he had bought some fowls from **Edward Bailey** at *"rather under value"* which may be hers. On the following Thursday Cuckney brought 3 or 4 fowls which Mrs Botting recognised as hers, and at Steyning the following morning she identified the remainder. John & Elizabeth Botting ordered the Constable of the Hundred of Steyning to be in readiness the next morning to apprehand Edward Bailey - who was taken before **Mr Goring** of Wiston who committed him for trial and bound over John & Elizabeth Botting to prosecute and Cuckney to give evidence.

William Paskins will swear that he saw Cuckney buy the fowls.

Receipt for expenses in this case;

Mr John Botting	dr to John Cuckney
Horses & self's	16s. 6d
Horse hire two days	14s.
My time two days	4s.
My Sister's time two days	2s
(Total)	£1.16s. 6d

February 2nd - receipted John Cuckney

Discussion in the marketplace - W.H. Pyne *(Etchings of Rustic Figures)*

---

[18]   A Higler was a man who bought fowls direct from the farmer to forestall the market.

Horsham Museum MSS Cat. No. 385, *extracted by Audrey Goffe*

The King (on the Prosecution of Mr. Charlwood Hammond) against John Boxall

Sussex, Easter Sessions 1800

Indictment against John Boxall late of Thakeham, Lath Cleaver, for feloniously breaking open the Prosecutor's Mill at Pulborough on the 9th March last and Feloniously taking and carrying away from thence One Hempen Sack of the value of Two shillings and Two Bushels and an half of Flour contained therein of the value of 50s., the property of Richard Moase, and one other Hempen Sack of the value of Two shillings and Two Bushells of Flour contained therein of the value of 40s., the property of William Greenfield.

The case for the prosecution

William White, who has for considerably more than 20 years worked as a Miller for the Prosecutor (**Mr. Charlwood Hammond**), left Nep Bourn Lower Mill in the parish of Pulborough about 7 o'clock in the evening of the 8th March last and, at that time, the Sack of **Richard Moase**, marked "H. Harding", with two bushels and an half of flour, and the Sack of **William Greenfield** marked "W. Greenfield", with two bushels of Flour, were in the Mill.[19] On his return to work at the Mill about six o'clock the following morning, viz. the 9th March, he found the Mill door open, which he discovered had been effected by breaking part of the window contiguous to the Door and opening the Bolt of the door and immediately missed the Sacks with their contents. He took the first opportunity to inform his Master, who caused the robbery to be advertised with a Reward of Ten guineas for the discovery of the offender.

On the 15th March **Mr. John Chatfield** of Thakeham Place, on passing a pond near his house, discovered something floating near the surface of the water, which he at first took for a fish. On procuring a hook or pole, he with considerable difficulty got out of the pond a sack marked "H. Harding" and within the same part of another sack with the mark, "W. Greenfield" thereon and some large stones obviously intended to sink them to the bottom of the pond. The house nearest the pond is that of the prisoner, **John Boxall**, and he *"being a very Suspicious Character"*, Mr. Chatfield went the next day (the 13th) to Mr. Hammond the Prosecutor to inform him of having found the sack and piece of another, and his suspicions of the prisoner. Mr. Hammond being gone to Horsham market, Mr. Chatfield sent him a note desiring to see him, and on the following day the prosecutor went to Mr. Chatfield, who shewed him the sack and the piece which he had found. Mr. Hammond took them home with him and on producing them to William White, his Miller, he well remembered the Marks and knew them to be the property of Greenfield and Moase. On the 17th March, Mr. Hammond went to Horsham and obtained a Warrant to search the prisoner's house and the same afternoon accompanied by **William Langley**, a peace officer, went to Thakeham and searched such house accordingly and found there a piece of sack which exactly matched the peace found in the pond marked, "W. Greenfield" and also about three bushels of flour in the house, viz. about a bushel in a Baking Kiver *(a mashing vat)* about another bushel in a sack just by, and in a Back Room under 3 tubs in a Brew Vat about another bushel in a bag, whereupon they took the prisoner into custody. Accompanied by William White, the Miller, and the said William Greenfield, they brought him before **Mr. Tredcroft** at Horsham, who committed him to Horsham Gaol.

The prisoner Boxall has for several years past been suspected of committing robberies in the neighbourhood of Thakeham and, about four years ago, the Prosecutor Mr. Hammond's mill was broken open and he then suspected Boxall, because he used to bring wheat to grind at the Mill which was not clean as ought to be. On this suspicion, Mr. Hammond directed William White his Miller not to grind any more wheat that Boxall the prisoner should bring. At the last Michaelmas Sessions at Petworth, the prisoner was tried and convicted of stealing woollen collar cloth, which had been manufactured at the House of Industry at Thakeham, from the Drying Ground in the parish of Sullington, near to the said House of Industry. He was sentenced to six weeks imprisonment for the said offence. *Document endorsed:* Convicted: 2 months imprisonment and twice publickly whipped.

---

[19] Sussex Record Society, Vol. 82, *West Sussex Land Tax 1785*, Pulborough pp. 182-5. Though William White can be found in Pulborough in the 1785 Land Tax records, Charlwood Hammond and Richard Moase both lived in West Chiltington at that time (pp. 88-89).

Chesworth (vignette by H.S. Syms from *Horsham; Its History and Antiquities*
by Dorothea Hurst, first published in 1865**)**

Engraving of duck - Thomas Bewick

Horsham Museum MSS Cat. No. 394, *extracted by Audrey Goffe.*

The King (on the Prosecution of Mr. George Brooke) vs Thomas West (a prisoner)

Horsham Sessions 1801

Indictment against Thomas West, late of Horsham, Labourer, for stealing eleven duck eggs the property of Mr. George Brooke from a Farm called Cheesworth Farm in his occupation in the Parish of Horsham on the 16th April last.

The case for the prosecution (brief - Mr. Newland)

On Thursday 16th April 1801 between five and six o'clock in the afternoon as the prosecutor, **Mr. George Brooke,** was walking round his grounds and going towards a Barn called the Hovel Barn, he saw the Prisoner (accompanied by his Boy) approach him and observed the Prisoner put some Eggs into his Bosom. The prosecutor immediately met the prisoner and said, *"West, take those Eggs out."* The prisoner making no answer the Prosecutor again said, *"Take those Eggs out. I saw you put them in your Bosom."* The prisoner then took from his Bosom six Duck Eggs. The Prosecutor said, *"That is not all".* West then took out two more Duck Eggs but, the Prosecutor believing the prisoner had more, insisted on his producing the rest. And then the prisoner drew out three more making in the whole Eleven. Just as the Eggs had been delivered to the Prosecutor, a Person of the Name of Penfold (a labouring man residing at Southwater in Horsham) came along and went with the Prosecutor, the Prisoner and his Boy, to a nest where a Duck was sitting near the spot, and on Lifting up the Duck, not a single Egg remained under her. The Prosecutor then restored the Eggs to the nest and told the prisoner he should get a warrant for him. The prisoner begged he would not, and Mr. Brooke permitted the prisoner at that time to depart.

On the following day the Prosecutor, hearing that the prisoner had a Wife and Family and was a Parishioner of Rudgwick, told him he must return with his family to Rudgwick. The Prosecutor not seeing or hearing any thing of the prisoner on the Monday or Tuesday following, imagined he was gone with his Family to Rudgwick, but on the Thursday following learnt that he remained at his former Residence, at a place called Grub Street on Horsham Common.

The next morning (Friday) the Prosecutor, on going to the duck's Nest, missed the duck and all the eggs and, suspecting the prisoner had stolen them, obtained a Warrant, in consequence of which he was apprehended and committed to Petworth House of Correction to take his Trial for stealing the eleven Duck Eggs as before stated.

Mr. George Brooke, the Prosecutor, will prove these circumstances and **Henry Penfold** will prove his accompanying him to the Duck's nest and that no Eggs were under her.

(*Document endorsed*: GUILTY a fortnight to Petworth. Had been there from 25th April last).

Horsham Museum MSS Cat. No. 404, *extracted by* **Sheila Stevens**

The King (on the prosecution of Mr William Stanford) vs Joseph Pierce (a prisoner) for felony.

Horsham Midsummer Sessions 1803

Indictment against Joseph Pierce for feloniously stealing 10 ells of Linen Cloth on the 21ˢᵗ June last at the Parish of West Grinstead of the value of *(blank space)* the property of Mr William Stanford.

The case for the prosecution

The prosecutor, **Mr William Stanford**, who is a considerable farmer in the parish of West Grinsted, sometime prior to the month of June last, delivered to **Richard Stringer** (the Governor of the workhouse at West Grinstead) a pair of new wove sheets, containing about 10 ells of linen cloth, for the purpose of being whited or bleached. When the linen was so delivered it was marked at each end or corner of both sheets with the initials W S. In the evening of the 21ˢᵗ of June last the said Richard Stringer missed the sheets from his premises and, suspecting they were stolen, went the following day to the prosecutor's house. He told his wife of the circumstance in the absence of her husband at Horsham market. On Mr. Stanford's return, he sent for Stringer & conversed with him on the subject, but they did not, at that time, suspect any particular person of the robbery.

The prisoner **Joseph Pierce**, who was a pauper at West Grinstead workhouse, had frequently in the summer gone away on the tramp and, on the 24ᵗʰ day of June (3 days after the robbery), applied to Stringer to permit him to be off again & to be allowed to take his cloths *(sic)* with him. Stringer accompanied the prisoner to Mr Nailard, one of the parish officers, to consult him as to letting him take his clothes with him, which was consented to on the prisoner's promising not to be a burthen on the parish for a limited time. The prisoner & Stringer then separated, the former saying he should go near London to haymaking, but after taking a circuit round by Henfield in a contrary direction, came back to West Grinstead and then took the London Road. Stringer now had some suspicion against the prisoner. **John Tubb**, a miller at West Grinstead, *(who presumably acted as the parish constable)* hearing that Pierce was gone through West Grinstead Park with a bundle tied in his round frock (smock) pursued him. On enquiry, Tubb found that the prisoner had deviated from the direct road and gone towards Shipley workhouse. As soon as Tubb came up to the prisoner, he clapped him on the back and insisted on seeing the contents of his bundle. On searching the same, he found a quantity of home made cloth with all the corners cut off, and then took him into custody and conducted him back to Stringer who, as well as Mr Stanford, identified the cloth found upon him to be the prosecutor's property. The next day the prisoner was taken before **Mr Tredcroft** *(the chief magistrate in Horsham)* who committed him to Petworth charged with the felony.

Proofs for the Prosecutor   *(Note on the cover -* Brief for the prosecutor Mr Courthope)

To prove the delivery of the cloth to Stringer to be bleached its being)
marked with his initials W S at the corners and that the cloth found   ) **Mr Wᵐ Stanford**
upon the prisoner is his property   Call   )   the prosecutor
To prove that the cloth found on the prisoner was the same which was delivered)
to him by the prosecutor and stolen from the premises whilst bleaching -- that)
the marks of the four corners (W S) were cut off – two of which marks were   ) **Richᵈ Stringer**
afterwards found in the place where the prisoner had secreted the sheets when   )
first stolen and exactly tally with the other part of the sheets where cut   Call)
To prove that he pursued and overtook the prisoner near Shipley workhouse and on)
Searching his bundle found the sheets (which will be produced) with the corners cut off Call) **John Tubb**

Editorial comment; In Thomas Charles Medwin's ledger for 1798-1808 (HM MSS Cat. No. 298) there is a note saying that Pierce was convicted and sentenced to 12 months' imprisonment at Petworth.

Horsham Museum MSS Cat. No. 425, *extracted by Sheila Stevens*

The King (on the prosecution of Mr Samuel Rowland) v John Shine for felony.

Chichester Epiphany Sessions 1808

(Note on the document - Transported for 7 years. Mr Courthope   2gns).

The case for the prosecution

The prisoner was committed to Petworth Gaol sir, to be indicted at this session for feloniously stealing on the 17th of June last from New Lodge, the mansion house of Mr Aldridge at the Parish of Beeding at Seal, 36lbs of lead, the property of Samuel Rowland and John Savage.

The prosecutor, **Samuel Rowland**, is a stone mason at Horsham and having in conjunction with **John Savage** of the same place, carpenter, undertook to new heal[20] New Lodge House (in which contract the lead and the old materials of the roof were to be their property) employed the prisoner, **John Shine** as a slater to assist in the work.   In the month of June the prosecution missed, from off the house, a considerable quantity of lead at different times and was led to suspect some of the workmen of stealing the same, but not knowing whom in particular to suspect, he had not taxed any one of them openly with it but said generally to the workmen *"some of you steal my lead".*

Finding his loss more considerable every day, he determined to remove the lead to a place of safety in his own house and took a cart load of lead away immediately.   Thinking it might lead to a discovery of the offender, he started going to the different plumbers in the town of Horsham to enquire if any of them had bought lately any quantity of lead.   As he went from his house he met **Henry Murrell**, a plumber and glazier of Horsham.   Murrell asked him if he had not lost some lead for he had bought some from Shine, one of his workmen.   He also said that Shine had come a second time to his shop with another parcel, and said he would go home and get the remainder of the lead he had to sell.

When he first came to the shop, there was only **Daniel Richardson,** then his apprentice, but on Shine's return with the last parcel, Murrell came in and refused to buy any more of him, asking him how he came by it and whether he got it honestly?   Shine swore he did, that he had had it by him from an old job.   Murrell told him he would buy no more of him and almost kicked him out of his shop.   Shine then took the lead, tied up in a cloth, to Howes's at the Crown Inn, Horsham to go by the Brighthelmstone coach on the Monday morning.

Samuel Rowland on the evening of Saturday, after he had paid his other workmen, called Shine into his back room alone and said to him; *"Shine, I am sorry for what I am going to tell you - you have been robbing me - you have sold some and offered some more of my lead for sale at Murrell's".*   Shine denied it and swore he had not.   Rowland asked him if he had not taken any lead to the Crown?   Shine replied that he had brought some lead from Brighton.   Rowland asked him if he wanted any money for his work.   He said he wanted £2 which his master gave him.   *(Note in the margin;* this was before he charged him with the theft).

Besides the lead sold to Murrell, the prisoner brought a large quantity tied up in a dirty cloth to the Crown Inn, Horsham, kept by **Harry Howes**.   The parcel was given in to the care of **Jane Peters**, a servant at *The Crown,* who told her master of it and he informed the prosecutor of the circumstance and who, on seeing the lead, knew it to be his property and this lead will be produced in court and sworn to.   The parcel of lead sold to Murrell was first delivered to Daniel Richardson, Murrell's apprentice, and was soon afterwards melted down, but not before Rowland had seen it and known it to be part of the lead stolen as before mentioned.   **Thomas Hughes**, who worked with the prisoner at New Lodge, will relate that the prisoner endeavoured to persuade him to be concerned in the theft.   All the witnesses mentioned above will give evidence.

---

20   Repair of a roof made of Horsham stone was called "stone healing."

Horsham Museum MSS Cat. No. 492, *extracted by* **Norman Hewell**

The King vs Milford Mitchell for theft of a gun from Philip Chasemore

Midsummer Sessions at Horsham – 1833

Case for the prosecution

The Indictment states that prisoner, late of the parish of Horsham in the county of Sussex, labourer, on 5th day of February 1833 feloniously did steal take and carry away against the peace etc. one gun of the value of 5s, of the goods and chattels of Mr. Philip Chasemore.

The prosecutor, **Mr. Philip Chasemore**, is a farmer in the town of Horsham and, among other premises, is the owner and occupier of a farm situate on Horsham Common. In a granary on the farm he kept a gun for the purpose of destroying vermin and that gun was in its usual place in one of the bins on the 4th February last, as was observed by one of the workmen on the morning of that day;. He had occasion to go to the granary again between 4 and 5 o'clock in the afternoon and then saw that it was concealed behind some sacks and lying under the window. His suspicion was excited that something wrong had occurred and he put it back into the bin. He then locked the granary and took the key with him. On the following morning he found that the window of the granary had been opened and the gun in question stolen.

Some suspicion fell on a labourer named **Henry Huntley**, who was employed by Mr Chasemore on the premises. **Mr. Thomas**, the assistant overseer of Horsham, who had sent him to the prosecutor for work, went to his house and spoke to him of the loss of the gun and from what Huntley said was induced to search the house where the prisoner lodged. He went with Huntley to the house and on making enquiries, the prisoner's mother produced the gun which she brought out from a bedroom and handed over to Mr Thomas. Mitchell's accomplice Henry Huntley was taken into custody, and convicted of larceny at the last Quarter Sessions.

James Dale of Horsham, Sussex, labourer, gave evidence that he works and lives on Mr Chasemore's farm and that he was at the granary twice on the 4th February and saw and moved the gun and locked the granary and took the key. That he found the window was open on the next morning and that the gun was gone.

William Lanham Thomas of Horsham, Sussex, assistant overseer, gave evidence of his suspicions and his visit to Huntley's and Mitchell's houses and the production of the gun by Mitchell's mother, and said that he had sent Huntley to work for Mr Chasemore.

Henry Loxley, late one of the constables of the Borough of Horsham, gave evidence that he had a warrant at Petworth.

Mitchell eluded the vigilance of the constable until after he heard the sentence and, finding it was much lighter than he expected, he gave himself up. He was taken before the magistrates and committed for trial where he made the following written confession: -

> That Huntley had asked him when they went home if he would go for a walk. He asked where and was told to Mr Chasemore's farm at the *Dog and Bacon* Public House after his gun. Mitchell said he did not mind any thing about it, and when he got there he stood outside upon the road and Huntley said he would go and fetch it and he remained there till Huntley returned. He came with the gun on his shoulder. When he got down to the prisoner's lodgings he asked him to take care of the gun till morning and he would then come and take it. Prisoner said he had no objection to take it home, but his mother did not like to have a gun in the house. He went over to Carter's Lodge the next morning and when he came back Huntley was taken. He did not knew that the gun was stolen.

The constable Loxley went to arrest Mitchell but he had absconded and he eventually arrested him on Friday prior to his examination on 20th April last. Philip Chasemore identified the gun as being his property that was lost.

If it was thought necessary to help with the prosecution, then **Mr William Stedman**, the magistrate's clerk, would produce the prisoner's confession.

Mitchell was found not guilty.

Editorial comment:. William Lanham Thomas, who is mentioned here as an assistant overseer of the poor, appears to have been a strong and forceful character whose life in Horsham was somewhat varied in its success. He was most probably a nephew of Henry and John Lanham, both grocers from Wiltshire, whose sister Susannah married a John Thomas in 1785. John Lanham was responsible for launching the first two Horsham Banks; one failed during the general collapse of country banks in 1793, and the other went bankrupt in 1816. William must have followed his uncles to Horsham in search of opportunity, like many others at this time.

In about 1812 Lanham Thomas was first mentioned as "superintending" the Horsham National School, newly set up by the Rev. George Marshall, curate of Horsham, in the Trinity Chantry in St. Mary's Church., to give primary education to 100 boys. He performed this office "with great credit to himself" and, as a result, he was appointed as Usher (or second Master) of Collyer's School by the then Headmaster, the Rev. Thomas Williams, in 1813. Willaims and Thomas appear to have worked reasonably well together for several years, until they fell out in rather spectacular fashion in 1821. Lanham Thomas was not a university graduate and classical scholar like the Rev. Thomas Williams; he was a self-made man who ran several small businesses on the side; he kept a cow in the School croft, made brooms and ran a carrier's wagon to London. Williams felt that it was "an Incongruity that the Usher of the Free School should be seen in the Town with a smock frock unloading his Waggon" and tried to discipline him; but Lanham Thomas maintained that since he was separately elected, he had "the freehold of his Office" and could do as he pleased. The quarrel came to a head in January 1821 and raged for several weeks, despite an abortive attempt by the Headmaster and the Schoolwardens to suspend Lanham Thomas and appoint a new Usher, Robert Eason, (who is mentioned in case no. 429, in the Appendix). Lanham Thomas invaded the schoolroom in noisy protest to demand his rights, and the Headmaster had to close the school down until April. But the appointment of two new Schoolwardens with "radical" views strengthened Lanham Thomas's hand, and the Headmaster finally resigned in protest in December 1821, having signally failed to gain the complete authority he had sought over his Usher. The new young Headmaster, William Pirie, whose election was fiercely contested by some elements in the town, was saddled for a few months longer with Lanham Thomas, until he could be persuaded take up a new venture - a grocer's shop in Brighton. (There are extensive records of this dispute among the papers relating to Collyer's School held by the Mercers' Company - see A.N. Willson, A History of Collyer's School 1532-1964, pp. 123-131).

Maybe Thomas's departure from the School was finally achieved because he was also being pursued for a debt in his other career as a "common carrier" by John Heath, blacksmith, at the Horsham Borough Court in 1821. But Lanham Thomas was back in Horsham only a few years later, and it appears from the above court case that he was acting as an assistant overseer of the poor in 1833, despite the fact that he had been charged with assaulting James Agate, linen draper, during a brawl in the Anchor Inn in 1832 (HM MSS Cat. No. 644). He also is known to have built a stable or cowshed in Denne Road - now a cottage which bears his initials and the date 1836 - so it looks as if he was still running a business on the side. By 1839 he was described as a "yeoman" in a draft agreement with the parish officers, as incoming tenant of some parish land near the Dog and Bacon Inn (HM MSS Cat. No. 2115).- maybe his stint as assistant overseer had enabled him to gain this tenancy. He appeared in the 1841 Census as an "agriculturist", living in Walnut Lodge in North Parade. In the 1840 Tithe Map assessment it appears that Walnut Lodge was a house and garden with an attached orchard and meadow, barn and yard, tenanted by William Lanham Thomas, but now owned by Henry Padwick, the lawyer and moneylender, who was by then building up a property portfolio in Horsham The date of William Lanham Thomas's death is not known; he is buried in the churchyard of St. Mary's and his grave bears the date 1788 - but presumably this was the date of his birth. The remainder of the inscription is now illegible.

Horsham Museum MSS Cat. No. 493, *extracted by* **Norman Hewell**

The King vs Charles Oakes, for the theft of tobacco from Mr. William Lintott

Sussex Midsummer Sessions at Horsham – 1ˢᵗ July 1834

The prisoner is charged with stealing a small quantity of tobacco from the prosecutor, his late master, under the following circumstances;

Charles Oakes had lived in the service of **Mr Lintott**, who is a grocer carrying on an extensive trade at Horsham, for four years and for his service received his board and 7s. per week wages. He had lately become connected with a young woman, also in Mr Lintott's service. He was apprehensive about her being pregnant and had determined to avoid the consequences by leaving Horsham and seeking employment in America and he had, with the idea of more speedily acquiring the means of his proposed voyage, purchased some smuggled tobacco. He had placed a part of this in a warehouse loft on his master's premises, where he occasionally placed some of his clothes. About 11 o'clock on Saturday night 21ˢᵗ June he went to the loft for a pair of shoes and found that an orange box in which he had stored a parcel containing 7lbs tobacco, had been removed. The parcel had been taken out and was still there. He took the parcel and his shoes, tied up in a pocket handkerchief.

He wondered about the removal of the box and taking out his parcel so on the way home to his lodgings at the house of his uncle, **Mr George Oakes**, who was a grocer in a small business, living in a different part of the town, he called on **Stephen Stovell**, a fellow servant in Mr Lintott's employ, who lived in a house almost opposite to Charles Oakes' uncle and there carried on the same business as a grocer, and told him that he had got into trouble. Stovell said *"What is there somebody in the family way by you?"* Oakes said *"Yes, I am afraid there is something worse, did you go up to the loft for an orange box?"* *"I did not, the boy fetched it"* said Stovell. Oakes *said "I had a parcel up there and it has been moved, did you hear any talk of it?"* Stovell replied *"I have not, I saw the boy in the counting house talking to Mr Lintott and I thought the master was blowing him up!"* Oakes said *"I must be off then, the parcel I had there was tobacco which I was going to sell to my uncle. I told him about it a couple of nights ago and he agreed to take 7lbs of it. It is over in my uncle's back yard but it won't be there long!"* Oakes asked Stovell to lend him five shillings which Stovell gave him and then Oakes said *"I am for America, I must bolt."*

Oakes then went to his lodgings and borrowed £2 from his aunt and asked to be called at 4 o'clock in the morning as he was going to exercise his master's horse, a service he had performed on other occasions. He however left Horsham on that same night on his way to London. About a mile and a half from Horsham he threw the parcel into Warnham Mill Pool. Shortly after that he met **Henry Heath**, a carrier on his way from London to Horsham, and borrowed 2s.6d. for payment of which he referred him to his father, residing at Dorking. On reaching Dorking, he called on his father and told him that he was going to America on account of a young woman at Horsham who was in the family way by him, and that when he got to London he should go and see his cousin, **Sheppard Oakes**, at New Cross near Newington.

He went to London, which he reached on Sunday afternoon 22ⁿᵈ June, and on Monday 23ʳᵈ he hired a berth in a vessel bound for America, paying 20s on account of his passage money, and taking a receipt for the same. He also went to see his cousin, Sheppard Oakes, during the day. In the evening about 10 o'clock he was met in the Old Kent Road, in the direction of New Cross, by **Drew Honywood**, the book keeper belonging to the Horsham coach, who had been sent from Horsham to apprehend him. *"I suppose that is about the tobacco"* said Oakes. Mr Honywood said it was and that Mr Lintott wanted to know where it was. Oakes said it was in Warnham Mill Pool and he went willingly with Honywood, gave him all the remaining money that he had (£1.11s.1½d) together with the receipt for the money he had paid for his passage money to America. He was brought back to Horsham on Tuesday 24ᵗʰ and on Wednesday 25ᵗʰ examined before **Mr Aldridge** and committed for trial.

It seems that on Saturday night 21st June, Stovell, after lending Oakes 5s., went straight to Mr Lintott and told him what had passed, which enabled immediate action to pursue the prisoner.   Stovell however falsely asserted to Mr Lintott - it appears out of spite - that the prisoner had told him that he had carried out a system of robbery during all of the four years he had been in Mr Lintott's service and that his uncle had received the stolen property. In consequence, on Sunday morning 22nd June, Mr Lintott accompanied by his head shopman and by Stovell went to the house of the uncle and accused him generally of receiving property which had been stolen from Mr Lintott, particularly the 7lbs of tobacco. The uncle denied the accusation and produced about 14lbs of tobacco which he had in his shop, together with the invoices, and Mr Lintott was satisfied.

The evidence before the examining magistrate was as follows: -

Charles Yohurst, shop boy, said he found the parcel in the orange box on Saturday night. He left it there but it was missing later and it smelled like tobacco or snuff and weighed about 7lbs.

Esther Baker, servant girl, said that she heard Oakes on the stairs to the loft about 11 o'clock on Saturday night and that afterwards he brought a parcel through the kitchen, wrapped in a pocket handkerchief.

Stephen Stovell gave evidence as above but, being under oath, left out the information he had falsely given to Mr Lintott.

George Livrer, Miller at Warnham Mill, on 22nd June between 6 and 7 in the morning, saw a parcel lying in the shallow water, he fished it out. It was about 5 or 6lbs of tobacco.

William Weller, shopman to Mr Lintott, was sent to Warnham Mill on the morning of 23rd June and collected the wet tobacco. He had damped some of his uncle's tobacco and compared it.

Drew Honywood, book keeper of the London to Horsham Coach, gave evidence concerning the apprehension of Oakes. He described how he waited 5 hours at New Cross, and how the tobacco had been thrown into Warnham Mill Pool.

Henry Heath, Carrier, told how he saw Oakes on the London road between 12 and 1 o'clock. Oakes had asked for half a sovereign. He had lent him half a crown. Oakes had been quarter to half a mile from Warnham Mill on the London side.

Oakes was found guilty – imprisonment for 12 months with hard labour.

Man on the road - W.H. Pyne (*Etchings of Rustic Figures*)

Man leading horse - W.H. Pyne (*Etchings of Rustic Figures*)

Pease Pottage *(from The Brighton Road)*

The King vs Walter Williard (nephew) for theft of a horse from Mary Williard (Widow)

Spring Assizes at Lewes – 16th March 1840

The indictment states that **Walter Williard**, late of the parish of Shenfield in Essex, labourer, on 21st February 1840 at the parish of Beeding, otherwise Seale in Sussex, did feloniously steal, take and carry away, against the peace etc.,one gelding worth £25 of the goods and chattels of one **Mary Williard**.

The case for the prosecution

The prosecutrix is a farmer in humble circumstance, residing and carrying on business upon Lower Bewbush Farm in the parish of Beeding, otherwise Seale, in the County.[21] The prisoner's father is a farm labourer in the prosecutrix's employ, as an inmate of her house, and is her brother in law, namely, the brother of her deceased husband, and was for some years up to Michaelmas last, or thereabouts, her bailiff. The prisoner is a labourer and resides at Shenfield in Essex, distant about 50 miles via London from Lower Bewbush Farm, and was formerly a beershop keeper in Brighton. He has occasionally visited his father and his aunt at the farm and so had the means of becoming conversant with the buildings upon the farm and possibly of learning the quality of the horses kept and used upon it. He was seen at a public house on Ifield Green, distant about a mile and a half or two miles from Lower Bewbush Farm, in the preceding night on which the robbery occurred, and remained there for an hour or an hour and a half, leaving at dusk. He was subsequently seen, or rather a man dressed exactly as the prisoner had been, walking towards Lower Bewbush Farm.

The witness **Gasson**, who is the carter employed on the farm, left the prosecutrix's horses at about nine on the night of the robbery, safe in the stable, but on going there at about five on the following morning missed the horse in question. He describes the horse as a brown cart gelding with a white face, two white saddle marks, one on each side, one white foot and heel and several grey hairs in his mane and tail, and as the most valuable horse in his mistress's team. He found the chain, which had secured the door of the stable overnight, had been cut out of the door, the chain thus dropping and leaving the door open. He also found the top board of the window shutter, which he had secured overnight by a wooden peg through a staple on the inside, had been forced, leaving room for the hand and arm of a person to be able to undo the fastening. He tracked the horse from the stable door on to the Horsham and Crawley road and thence towards Crawley and London.

Between 11 and 12 o'clock on the same night, the witness, **Hards**, who keeps the tollgate on the Horsham and Crawley turnpike road, about a mile and a half distant from Lower Bewbush Farm and about half a mile from Crawley, was called by a person rapping at the door of the tollhouse. Hards got up and found a man at the gate, leading a carthorse with a white face. The man said, in a disguised gruff voice, that he was in a hurry and must get on. He had on a light coloured sort of shooting jacket, half laced boots and leather gaiters or leggings. (This dress corresponds to that which the prisoner wore when seen at Ifield Green as described by the witnesses, **Burberry** and **Denman**, agreeing also with the clothes in which he appeared before the committing magistrate). The horse had a halter on and a light coloured greatcoat thrown over his back, agreeing in description with one which the prisoner wore at Ifield Green and identified as similar to one obtained by the constable at the prisoner's lodgings on his arrest and produced before the committing magistrate. Hards opened the gate and let the horse through.

On the following day Hards heard of the robbery and also heard that Williard, with whom he is well acquainted, had been seen in the neighbourhood during the previous afternoon and he will swear that Williard is the man who he let through the tollgate with a horse. He will also state that he knows the prosecutrix's team of horses, having seen them frequently pass through his tollgate, and that the horse with the prisoner on the night in question was very like one of those he had noticed in the team.

---

[21] In 1840, the parish of Lower Beeding was created from the northern portion of the parish of Beeding, or Seale. The other part of the parish, some miles away, was then called Upper Beeding. At this time, it stretched up to Ifield in what is now the western part of Crawley.

About 12 o'clock on the night in question a man, wearing a light coloured great coat like the one already described, and leading a brown horse with a white face and a fairish tail, passed the tollgate at Crawley on the London and Brighton turnpike road towards London (distant about a mile from Hard's tollgate) and the witness **Gibson** in addition to his proof that the man so passed, will state that the horse hung back very much and seeming unwilling to pass through the gate, and that he, Gibson, suspected something amiss and asked the cause. The man said that he had left three other horses behind at Pease Pottage gate, where he had supped, that the horse with him did not like to go without the others, but that his helper would pass with them presently and he wished Gibson would hurry them along. In point of fact, no such horses did pass through the Crawley gate on that night. On enquiry from the landlord at the Pease Pottage gate, **Stanford Bartley**, another witness, he wholly falsified the prisoner's statement that he and his helper had supped at his house and were bringing with them three or four horses as alleged. He will also prove that the Pease Pottage gate is about three miles from Crawley on the main turnpike road towards Brighton, which is a different road from the Horsham and Crawley one.

About 2 in the morning after the robbery the prisoner was seen at the tollgate next to Reigate on the road through Sutton to London and about 10 miles beyond Crawley, by the witness, **Winch**, who is the guard of the Brighton and London Red Van,. He will give evidence that the prisoner accompanied his van from the last mentioned tollgate as far as Sutton, about 9 miles beyond Reigate, and that he rode a horse with a white face and wore a light coloured greatcoat. He afterwards proceeded with the van from Sutton to Tooting, about 5 miles further on the way to London and, on stopping at the *King's Head*, found the prisoner there, or rather, the same person who had accompanied him on horseback from Reigate to Sutton and who appeared to be known to and will be identified by the witness, **Charlwood**, as the prisoner. Between 5 and 6 in the morning after the robbery, the prisoner arrived at the *King's Head*, Tooting as already stated and Charlwood says that he had with him a brown cart horse, which had a white face and one white hind foot and fetlock, that he put the horse in the stable and came into the house where he stayed for about half an hour and then left, leading the horse, towards London. Whilst the prisoner was at the *King's Head*, the Brighton and London Red Van stopped at the door and the witness Winch came into the room where the prisoner was sitting, saw him and recognised him.

On 27th February, six days after the robbery, Williard was arrested at Shenfield in Essex and, as it would appear, was wearing the very same clothes in which he committed he robbery. He admitted having been down to Reigate and Ifield and West Green, which is close to Crawley, but on the Crawley side of Hards' turnpike gate and distant about half a mile. He admitted having a horse in his possession on the night of the robbery but made the usual thief's excuse that he was sent from London by a person whom he did not know, to take charge of some horses and he met a man, whom he also did not know, naming West Green as the place where they met, who placed the horse in his care. He added that he was to have had three or four more horses, but was disappointed, as they were not brought up and that if the horse in question was found, he could prove how he came by it. This might prove difficult as the horse has not been seen since the night it was stolen but it is hoped that, as normal, where the stolen property is found in the possession of an accused person, that it will be necessary for that person to prove his innocence, by producing the party or parties said to have employed him and so to have put the horse, seen to be in the prisoner's custody, into his hands. On that point, two points need to be borne in mind – first that the prisoner himself gave contradicting accounts as to the place from where he brought the horse ; he told the constable and the witness Mr Baker that the horse was delivered to him at West Green, but told the witness Gibson that he brought the horse from Pease Pottage gate, and secondly that both those accounts are untrue according to the evidence of Hards, Burberry, Denman and Bartley.

Evidence was given by the witnesses as follows:-

Henry Gasson, carter at Lower Bewbush Farm told how he had left the stable locked and found it broken into in the morning. He gave a clear description of the stolen horse and followed the tracks to the Horsham to Crawley road.

Elizabeth Burberry, widow, landlady of the public house at Ifield Green told how Williard was at the public house on the afternoon of 21st February and that he left about dusk and she gave a description of his clothing.

Thomas Denman, labourer, returning home from work at dusk, met the prisoner on the road which leads to Ifield Mill and thence to Bewbush Mill and then to Lower Bewbush Farm. He also described his clothing but did not see his face and cannot swear that it was Williard.

William Hards, Tollgate keeper on the Horsham and Crawley turnpike.
John Gibson, Tollgate keeper on the London and Brighton road.
Joseph Winch, Guard on the Brighton and London Red Van.
Timothy Charlwood, Ostler at the *King's Head*, Tooting.
All four of these gave evidence as previously stated.

Benjamin Bacon, Constable of the parish of Southweald in Essex, told how he arrested the prisoner under a warrant of Dr Robinson, on Thursday 22nd February at his lodgings at Shenfield. He informed Williard that he was arrested on a charge of stealing a horse at Beeding in Sussex and Williard said *"I do not know anything about it, I have not stolen any horse"*. The prisoner said in conversation afterwards that he had been down to Highgate or Reigate and that the horse he had been in possession of and had sold, had been handed to him by a person at West Green and he should have had three or more. He said *"If the horse is found, I can prove how I came by it, the person who brought the horse to me was a littlish man, and I sold the horse at Smithfield market on Monday last and if the horse I had was Mrs Williard's, I am certain I did not steal it and did not know it was hers"*. Bacon also stated that the greatcoat which he will produce in court was given to him by the prisoner's wife at his lodgings and she said it belonged to the prisoner.

Richard Grey Baker, Bailiff on Bewbush Farm, confirmed that Williard's father lives and works at the farm, that Williard lives at Shenfield in Essex and was a beer shop keeper in Brighton and that he occasionally visited his father and aunt at Bewbush Farm. On 21st February last, although he was known to be in the vicinity, he did not make an appearance to his relations at the farm. On information received, he went to Brentwood in Essex and obtained a warrant to arrest Williard. The prisoner then stated similar information as given to the constable, but added *"I do not know him, but I should know him if I saw him. I was then engaged to sell the horse and another in a chop[22] and drew £14 to boot"*. When asked what he did with the horse he had in chop, said *"I sold it at Romford"* and when asked to whom he said he did not know him, but would if he saw him. He said that the man who he had the chop with was a tall, thin, light man with a long fustian coat on. Baker said that he could not recollect that the prisoner knew the man that had sent him to get the horse, but he had sold the horse he had in chop to a man at Westminster Bridge and not at Romford as previously stated, but that there had been some conversation about Romford.

Stanford Bartley, landlord at the public house at Pease Pottage Gate, The Black Swan, told that he knows Williard well and he has stayed at his public house during the summer, but was not there on 21st February at any time day or night, with or without horses. He also explained the position of his tollgate on the Brighton to London road which is a different road from that which passes from Horsham to Crawley. All of the witness statements were sworn before **Mr. Robert Aldridge**, magistrate.

---

[22] "Chop" here means barter, or buy and sell - the original meaning of "chop and change" *(Shorter Oxford Dictionary)*

Horsham Museum MSS Cat. No. 507, *extracted by Norrman Hewell*

The Queen vs James Booker for theft of Horse Roller and Silver Spoon from Henry Padwick Esq.

Easter Sessions at Petworth – 15th April 1841

The case for the defence

The prisoner was a stable boy in the service of **Mr Henry Padwick** from April 1840 to January 1841. He received 2s.6d per week and occasionally his board. He had a companion, a younger boy, who used to visit him at his master's stables, and who is indicted together with him on one or both of the present charges. His name is **James Sadler**. On 14th January, Sadler sold a horse roller, not the subject of this case and for which there was no claimant, to **Mr Tolhurst,** a pawnbroker of West Street,[23] Horsham and on the following day took another horse roller, which is the subject of this indictment, to Mr Tolhurst and offered it to pawn. Mr Tolhurst stopped the transaction on suspicion of it being stolen and gave information to **Dr Coleman**,[24] in whose service Sadler had formerly lived. Tolhurst also gave information to **Gower**,[25] the policeman at Horsham. Gower apprehended Sadler who said that he had received the roller from the prisoner, **James Booker**. He then apprehended Booker who confessed at once.

On 16th January Booker and Sadler were taken before the bench of magistrates at the *Kings Head Hotel* and, on the evidence of Tolhurst and particularly Gower, both boys were committed for trial at the present sessions. They were both however granted bail to appear and take their trial. In the evening of the same 16th, Booker was taken into custody by **Charles Feist**,[26] the constable at Horsham, on a charge of stealing a silver teaspoon. Sadler had given evidence that the spoon had been seen in Mr Padwick's hay loft and Feist asked Booker where it was. Booker said that he had seen it one day when Sadler was with him, in the loft over the stable, that it was shown him by Sadler in a hole under the rafters, that Booker took it out and cleaned it afterwards put it on a beam in the loft. Booker said that Sadler should take it indoors, but Sadler wanted to pawn it. It was left on the beam while Booker and Sadler went to feed Mr Padwick's horse in a field adjoining the stable. Booker then took Feist into the loft and showed him the spoon on the beam and gave it to Feist. Booker then went with Feist to Mr Padwick's office and there Booker repeated what he had told Feist.

On 20th January Booker was taken before **Mr Aldridge**, the committing magistrate, at **Mr Stedman's**, the magistrate's clerk's office and, on the evidence of Mr Padwick's servants Robert and Emily, who had counted all the spoons and found them complete, about a fortnight previously, and the evidence of Feist, was committed to Petworth for trial, but about three weeks later was released on bail. Sadler, on being interviewed by Feist, said that the spoon may have been put there by **Gudgeon,** who preceded Booker in Mr Padwick's service.

It would appear that there is no chance to escape conviction on the first charge, but it is hoped that the punishment, from which his friends are desirous of saving him, will have the desired effect of recalling him to a sense of the value of that character which, but for his own future good conduct, he has forfeited.

Sentence   Roller – 14 days imprisonment and one private whipping.   Spoon – case not presented.

Editorial comment:. Henry Burstow said that "the first professional policeman at Horsham was Gower, whom we boys regarded - at first - with fear, appointed October 1839". *(William Albery, Recollections of Horsham, being the Reminiscences of Henry Burstow, p. 52).*

---

[23] John Tolhurst of West Street appears a currier in the 1841 Census, but people often combined two jobs at this time.

[24] Dr. William Thomas Coleman, M.D., lived in East Street in 1841.

[25] John Gower, Police Officer, lived in North Street, and was aged 33 (1841 Census).

[26] Charles Feist later became a "bum-bailiff" and the most hated man in Horsham, according to Henry Burstow. *(Reminiscences,* p. 53).

The Queen vs George Charman junior for theft of four sovereigns from Matthias Walker

Petworth Sessions – 6th April 1843

The case for the defence

In the evidence sworn before the committing magistrate it was shown that on 13th March 1843 the prosecutor, who is an ironmonger, missed four sovereigns from the till behind the counter in his warehouse and shop in Horsham. Between 1 and 2 o'clock in the afternoon of that day, the prisoner, **George Charman junior,** came to the shop and bought some gun caps. **John Tugwell,** another boy, who is a witness for the prosecution, came to the shop at or about the same time. According to his evidence, which is denied by George Charman, the prisoner was already in the shop when Tugwell arrived, and there was no other person present. One of the boys rang the bell which is attached to the entrance door and **Mr. Moon,**[27] who is **Mr Walker's** apprentice, came and served them. Once served, the prisoner left immediately followed by Tugwell.

At 11 o'clock that night, **Gower**, the police constable, arrested the prisoner at a play or performance which took place at the Hurst Arms, and searched him and found only 1d (one penny) upon him. On being charged with stealing the sovereigns, the prisoner said that he had not seen or touched them. Gower then took the boy to his father's house, told his father of the charge and left him in his father's care.

Another witness for the prosecution, **Charles Henley**[28], stated that between 9 and 10 on Sunday morning 19th March, Charman went to **Mr Neeves'**[29] shop and bought two horse balls for which he paid by changing a sovereign and that he was wearing a fustian jacket. Mr Neeves runs a chemist shop in West Street, Horsham. Gower, the policeman, again arrested Charman on Monday 20th March and told him he had changed a sovereign at Mr Neeves' shop and the prisoner strenuously denied it, so much so that his father took him to Mr Neeves' shop and asked if it was true that this boy had been on Sunday morning to buy horse balls and changed a sovereign. Mr Neeves said that the prisoner was not the boy, it was a shorter boy with a round frock. Mr Neeves confirmed this before the committing magistrate. He also confirmed that, as Henley had stated, a boy had exchanged a sovereign for horse balls, which the boy said were for John Langley.

Henry Langley, who is the ostler at the Kings Head, where the prisoner's father is one of the post boys, said that he had not sent the boy to Mr Neeves to get horse balls on Sunday morning, although he had done so on other occasions, and he had always brought the right change. He was asked if he had the Christian name of John as well as Henry, or was ever called John, to which he answered *'No'*.

Observations;

The entire case seems very weak apart from the fact that the witness Henley has known the boy all his life. It would be very difficult for anyone at the front of the shop to get to the till, especially not to be noticed in the middle of the day. The shop is wholesale as well as retail and there are customers in and out all the time. The shop and warehouse is a passage and workmen employed by Mr Walker pass to and from the workshop all day long. The only way to reach the till, which is by a window behind the counter, is through a door from Mr Walker's house or from an opening far back in the warehouse.

Editorial comment: Although George Charman, aged sixteen, was acquitted of this offence, he was committed for trial a month later, on 27 May 1843,   charged with stealing 1s.6d from Miss Anne Ireland, who kept a shop in West Street. He was tried on 29 June at Horsham Sessions, and on this occasion he was sentenced to be transported for 7 years. (West Sussex Record Office, Quarter Sessions Index). There is a letter from his father, George Charman senior, to the Duke of Richmond among the Goodwood papers, as follows;

---

[27]   James Moon, aged 15, is shown in the 1841 census as an ironmenger's apprentice.

[28]   Charles Henley is described as an agricultural labourer in the 1841 Census, living in a lodging house.

[29]   Benjamin Neeves is listed as a druggist (chemist) in West Street in the 1841 Census.

"Having had a son named George Charman tried at the last Horsham Quarter Sessions for stealing three sixpences, the property of Miss Anne Ireland of this place, and for the said offence was Transported for Seven years and is now on board the York hulk at Portsmouth, Mr. Johnson, the counsel who defended him has written and informed me that you was so kind as to say that you would speak to Mr. Prime on behalf of my son. Your answer will extremely oblige Your obedient servant, George Charman, his father, Post Boy, King's Head Inn. (Goodwood MSS 1652, f. 392).

(This information came from notes on the Charman family made by John Charman, a copy of which was kindly given to Horsham Museum Society)

Post-boy - Bowes and Carver

Brewing using a copper - W.H. Pyne *(Microcosm)*

80

The Queen vs Thomas Coles, Henry Read and Peter Kensett for stealing a copper from Richard Baker

Petworth Sessions – Thursday 2nd January 1845

The case for the prosecution

The prosecutor, Richard Baker, is a farmer residing at Cowfold in this county. The prisoners are already pending for trial at the present sessions on several other prosecutions and in particular, the prosecution of Mary Burdfield, Widow. The charge is the same as this, against the prisoners Coles and Read, for stealing a copper fixed in the brickwork of a building (being a brewhouse) and as against the prisoner Kensett that he received such copper, knowing it to have been stolen.

Mr Baker's prosecution was instituted in consequence of circumstances disclosed by evidence from Mrs Burdfield's case. The copper was stolen at Cowfold in the night between 23rd and 24th October last, is supposed to have been sold by Coles or Read to Kensett at Billingshurst, which is about 10 miles distant from Cowfold, on 26th or 28th October, and will be proved to have been found in Kensett's hands on 4th November. Coles and Read were trampers (sic) and it is only fair to them to state that they were not seen in that neighbourhood of Cowfold for several days prior to the robbery. Their guilt is shown mainly, if not entirely, by their separate confessions taken before the committing magistrate.

The case against **Peter Kensett** is as follows: -

In the month of July last, a person was arrested at Billingshurst, upon whom a copper was found under suspicious circumstances, which he stated he was about to sell to Kensett and which copper was later discovered to have been stolen at Betchworth in Surrey. The witness, **Charles Feist**, verbally, and the witness **John Coppard Gower**, by a written communication, cautioned this prisoner against the purchase of copper or other similar articles for the future, as mischievous to the public and likely to involve himself and his family in danger, if persisted in. On being so cautioned, the prisoner promised to be very careful in all his subsequent dealings for such articles and to give notice to the police if any were brought to him for sale.

In a conversation with Gower on Monday 4th November, with reference to a copper which Kensett had left behind him at Billingshurst, and which afterwards proved to be the copper in question in this prosecution, Kensett falsely said he had brought it a month ago. In his examination before the committing magistrate on the same 4th November upon **Mrs Burdfield's** charge, he falsely stated that he had purchased only one copper in the last three or four months, until he bought the one which he then produced. That one was a 20 gallon copper which he further falsely alleged he had purchased from Coles on 2nd November, although it will be proved that beside three coppers and a brass boiler, voluntarily produced by him, 13 other coppers were found concealed, in his possession, and amongst them, the copper stolen from Mrs Burdfield (being a 40 gallon copper which he must have actually have purchased from Coles on 2nd November) and although he admitted by letter to Gower that he had not a single copper in his possession on 24th July, and Gower took possession of the copper on the evening of 4th November, Kensett repeated his former false statement that he had bought it a month or more before, although it was only stolen on 24th October; i.e. a week previously.

Evidence was given by **Richard Baker**, Farmer of Cowfold, that a copper was stolen from his brewhouse on 24th October and that a rivet given to him by Gower who had received it from **Hillman**, fits the copper which he believes to be his.

Sarah Woolven, single woman of Cowfold, is 21 years old and has lived in Mr Baker's service for more than 10 years. She went to the brewhouse before 6 am and found the door which had been secure between 7 pm and 8 pm on the previous evening, broken open, the lock was bent double and the copper was missing. She identified the copper, which she has frequently used and cleaned, by the black marks at the bottom.

Mary Akehurst, wife of John Akehurst, has worked as a charwoman at Mr Baker's house at Cowfold for 32 years, the last 12 for Mr Baker and the previous 20 for his uncle. She identified the copper which she has often used for washing and brewing, by the extra width and thickness of the rim, the colour of it and from a mark burnt at the bottom.

Mr Peter Hillman, labourer of Cowfold gave evidence that on 29th October, the Tuesday after the robbery he was at Peacock Hill between Cowfold and Billingshurst and he saw the remains of a fire at the side of the road, a smut on the ground and canker and marks which appeared to be from driving something into the ground. He also picked up a piece of rivet and found a sledge hammer with marks of canker upon it.

Edwin Kensett, shopkeeper, stated that he was Peter Kensett's son and that Read came to his father's shop on about 24th October and brought something covered with a wrapper. He did not see what it was but the wrapper was large enough to cover a copper doubled up, and it is usual to bring coppers when large in a wrapper for convenience of being carried. He said that Read left what he had brought and it was taken into the warehouse to be weighed, being large.

Mr Charles Feist, former constable of the Borough of Horsham, gave evidence about the theft last July of a copper from Betchworth in Surrey and of the caution given to Peter Kensett.

John Coppard Gower, Police Constable of the Borough of Horsham, gave evidence that on Sunday 3rd November, Peter Kensett came to Gower's house to enquire whether or not two men had been arrested regarding a stolen copper as he had brought a 20 gallon copper on Saturday morning. Gower said that a 40 gallon copper had been stolen from Cowfold and asked where the one which Kensett bought came from. Kensett said that it came from Toat Hill and that the men had been traced to Billingshurst and he thought that they had been arrested. Kensett said that the copper he had was not big enough by 10 or 15 gallons and he did not see how they can be found guilty as no one had seen them take it. If they are the men who stole it, perhaps they met someone and changed coppers like they do horses sometimes! Gower said he knew nothing about it and Kensett went home.

On the next day, Monday 4th November, Gower met Kensett again at the examination of Coles, Read and another person called Butler (who has since been discharged) on a charge of stealing Mrs Burdfield's copper. Gower said *"Have you brought the copper which you purchased from these two on Saturday morning?"* Kensett said that he had and they fetched it from his gig. Gower said *"This is not a forty gallon copper, but it's more than twenty gallons, I am told that you have a copper which is the right size, but you will not produce it!" "That's right"* said Kensett, *"I bought that a month ago, if Mrs Burdfield had kept quiet, I have no doubt that her copper would have been brought to me".* During the examination Kensett said *"I only bought one copper in the last three months".* Gower said *"Mr Kensett, you know that I was able to trace stolen property to your shop, more than three months ago".* Kensett said *"I did not know that".* Gower replied *"Yes you did, you wrote a letter about it, which I can produce".* Kensett said *"I have only purchased one copper during the last three or four months and that was from Coles, I gave him 2 or 3 shillings for it and if I found that his story was right, then he should come back in a few days. I made enquiries and found it was alright, that was why I bought the copper from him on Saturday morning".* Kensett was asked from whom he made enquiries and he said he had forgotten as it was so long ago, but it was some person at Chiddingfold.

That evening Gower went to Kensett's shop to see any coppers there, and two coppers and a brass boiler were produced. One looked like Mrs Burdfield's copper and Kensett confirmed that he had bought that more than a month ago. Gower said *"I do not know, but no one would like to suppose that a person of your standing in society would buy property that was stolen if you knew it to be stolen. I have authority from the magistrates to look at your coppers and I should like to take this one. I will call for it on my way back from Petworth."* He returned with another constable called **James Flanagan** and they searched the premises. In a large cask in the warehouse they found three coppers and two brass furnaces, two of the coppers, one of which looked nearly new, were broken into pieces. Kensett said *"I really had forgotten that they were there"* and after more conversation, Flanagan left and Gower took the copper which is the subject of this prosecution.

On Wednesday 6th November as a result of information received, Gower set out for Billingshurst and on the way between Horsham and Billingshurst passed Kensett going the other way. He turned back and caught up with Kensett and searched the cart, which appeared to have the springs weighed down, and found two coppers which Kensett denied were there. Gower said *"I shall take possession of these coppers, cart and all in the Queen's name, you had better drive me back to Billingshurst"*. Some argument followed, during which Gower said he had heard that Kensett had been removing coppers from his premises and Kensett said it was only the two old ones which he did not want on his premises. They returned to Billingshurst and went to the house of **George Belchambers**. Belchambers came to the door and Kensett told him they wanted the two old coppers he had left there. Gower said he had come to search the house and was shown into a dark room where he found one copper and one brass furnace. Gower called for a light and asked how many more coppers Belchambers had. He said he had two and Gower asked if that was two besides the two he had just seen. Belchambers confirmed this and they went to a room in the attic which was off a bedroom and there found four coppers. These coppers were all hidden in sacks. Gower arrested Kensett.

Thomas Lomas, Copper Smith, gave evidence that he restored the copper, in this case, as it had been beaten out of shape while it was heated, and that it is a 40 gallon copper which weighs 52 pounds (the weight of a copper is about a pound and a quarter per gallon), and that it is in too good a state to be sold as old metal.

Mr Pilfold Medwin, Solicitor for the prosecution, produced a duplicate of the notice served on Kensett's solicitors.

Sussex   **The Queen on the prosecution of**
Petworth Sessions   **Richard Baker against Thomas Coles,**
January 1845   **Henry Read and Peter Kensett**

I do hereby give you notice to produce in evidence on the trial of an indictment to be preferred in this prosecution at the next General Quarter Sessions of the Peace to be holden at Petworth in and for the western division of the said County of Sussex on Thursday the second day of January one thousand eight hundred and forty five, all day books, account books or books of entry, paper writings or memoranda belonging to and in the possession or power of you the above named Peter Kensett and kept or used by you between the first day of July one thousand eight hundred and forty four and the fourth day of November in the said last mentioned year inclusive.
Dated the 30th day of December 1844

To the above named   Pilfold Medwin
Peter Kensett and all others   Solicitors for the Prosecution
whom it may concern

The following is a letter written to Gower by Kensett in reply to Gower's letter of which no copy was kept.

                                                  Billingshurst, July 24th 1844
Dear Sir

In answer to yours I beg to say the coppers I have bought lately have been very old with one exception, concerning which I had some suspicion and told the parties for the future I should require a certificate, to which they said they had no objection. I have only one old brass kettle by me at present, except small things, having sent my mettles to the foundry. I do not expect much during the harvest but will give a good look out.

                    Yours truly Peter Kensett

William Smith Stedman Esquire, Clerk to the Horsham Bench of Magistrates, produced the original voluntary statements given by Read and Coles on 14th November 1844 before the committing magistrate, **James Tudor Nelthorpe**, Esquire.

Read said *"I am guilty of selling it but not guilty of stealing it".*

Coles said *"The first copper that I ever stole was two from Mrs Brown of the Crab Tree. Them I took to Mr Kensett myself and I received eighteen shillings and eleven pence, that was the value - seventeen shillings he paid me and he kept back one shilling and eleven pence because he said I had not come honestly by them. He said he had a caution from Horsham and he must be careful what he bought. I told him he had no call to fear for I had them in my possession two days, I think that was 11ᵗʰ October. The next time I went in company with Read and Read took a brass boiler which we stole from Mrs Moody of Rusper at the beer house. We were there drinking the Saturday and stole it on Sunday night or Monday morning. The coppers now marked No 1 I stole myself and sold myself. That is Mrs Moody's copper marked Moody No 2, that was sold to Mr Kensett for eight shillings and I think fourpence. The next time Read and me went in company and stole a copper which I think is the copper Mr Flanagan accuses Butler and me of stealing, but Butler is innocent. Read sold that to Mr Kensett for six and twenty shillings and fourpence. The copper marked Bellamy No 3 is the same copper. The next one Read and me stole was from Mr Baker. That I sold to Mr Kensett for five and twenty shillings and two pence halfpenny, weighing fifty three pounds. The copper marked Baker No 4 is the same copper. The next one we stole was from an empty house just out of Horsham that Read sold to Mr Kensett for thirteen shillings and eightpence weighing thirty pounds. The copper marked Holmes No 5 is the same copper. The next copper we stole from Itchingfield, I sold that to Mr Kensett for six and twenty shillings and eightpence weighing fifty six pounds or more, but that was the money I got for it. I told Mr Kensett I bought it the other side of Chiddingfold. The copper marked Burdfield No 6 is the same copper. There is one piece more I stole some long time ago from North Chapel just above the school. The piece of copper marked Northchapel is the same. The other pieces of copper came from the Parson's at Lurgashall, they were stolen by a man they call Bargeman Jack and a man they call Big Davey. A Brass Furnace marked Dunsill, Tickners Heath was stole by Bargeman Jack."*

Both statements were signed at the bottom by the prisoner concerned and by **Mr Nelthorpe**.

Editorial comment.   This case appears to owe much to the dogged police work of Police Constable Gower! Gower has been mentioned previously in two previous cases, as Horsham's first professional policeman.   It is clear that there was now a need for a modern police service, as opposed to the former system of amateur parish constables, who - though paid for the time lost from their normal jobs - were pressed into the service of the community by the Parish Vestry.

Rider and cart, W.H. Pyne *(Etchings of Rustic Figures)*

℘ Appendix - William Cooper, and the cases concerning him ℘

Among the records of the court cases found among the papers of Thomas Charles Medwin, there are several in which he clearly took an especial interest, as they concerned his former servant, William Cooper, who later became the landlord of the *Green Dragon*, in the Bishopric. Medwin served as his friend and lawyer during his lifetime, and then became his executor and trustee. He was thus involved in a long-running Chancery dispute concerning William Cooper's estate, which appears to have dragged on from 1807 until 1811 or later (as so many cases in Chancery did). But among the papers relating to the Chancery proceedings are several documents which illuminate the earlier cases in which Cooper had been involved during his lifetime. The two men had had a close relationship for many years, and it seems likely from the evidence of his gravestone that William came into Medwin's service as a young lad, aged about fourteen. From the evidence given in one of the cases (HM MSS Cat. No. 412) we know that Cooper was in Medwin's service for about 15 years, from about 1776 to 1791, and was then landlord of the *Green Dragon* in the Bishopric for 13 years, from about 1791 until the case was heard in 1804. He died in late 1805, and an inventory of the *Green Dragon* was carried out in January 1806.

William Cooper is almost certainly buried in St. Mary's churchyard, near the south western corner of the church. Only his name is now faintly visible - the rest of the inscription has disappeared. In the list of monumental inscriptions drawn up by Gordon Slyfield many years ago, when the inscriptions were in a much better state of repair, the date of his death was given as 1803. However, this is likely to be a simple error in transcription - 1803 instead of 1805 when we know that he died. He is said to have been aged 43 at the time of his death, which indicates that he was born in about 1762, but there is no record of his parents' marriage or his baptism in the Horsham records, and I have not yet been able to establish it elsewhere, with any certainty.

It seems from papers relating to a dispute over a pew in the church[30] that William Cooper was the son of a Thomas Cooper, who was a butcher, and his wife Jenny, the daughter of Richard Cock, tallowchandler, of an old Horsham family, who was entitled to one of the pew seats in the *"little south aisle"*. It is not quite clear whether Thomas Cooper was one of the Horsham Coopers, of whom there were several families, or whether he came from elsewhere - it is a common name and difficult to pin down. Mrs. Cooper moved away from Horsham to Battle for some years, which suggests that her husband might have come from there, but she later returned and reclaimed the pew from Mrs. Annie Oakes, whom she had allowed to use it while she was away, for her own use and that of her son. Thomas Charles Medwin, as an incomer to Horsham, needed the status symbol of his own pew in the church, and it it therefore not surprising that he managed to persuade old Mrs. Cooper and William to sell him their pew space, as it seems that in her final years Mrs. Cooper was in need of financial support. There is a bill from Henry Charman of £10.15s. for board and lodgings for the *"late Mrs. Cooper"* (mother of William) from 1795 to 1800 *"so that she should not live in the poor house"*.[31] But William himself seems to have acquired enough money to lease or property, in Warnham and Cowfold, and set up as an innkeeper, by this time.

Thomas Charles Medwin's first official appointment, as a young lawyer, was in 1776, as Receiver of Rents for his first cousins, the two orphaned heiresses of Warminghurst Park, Ann Jemima and Patty Butler. (Their mother Martha was the sister of Medwin's mother, Jane, and both were daughters of the Rev. Thomas Dolben, Rector of Wexham and Vicar of Stoke Poges in Buckinghamshire). Medwin was able to combine this post with setting up a lawyer's office in Horsham, since many of the properties which belonged to the Butler sisters were in the Horsham area. In the early 1780s, Ann Jemima Butler married the Rev. Roger Clough, while her younger sister Patty married Richard Clough of Plas Clough in Denbigh, Roger's older brother, and both sisters then moved to Wales. They left Thomas Charles Medwin as steward of their extensive Sussex estates, responsible for renting out Warminghurst Park and taking care of their farms and manors, which he did faithfully for the next twenty-five years, until Warminghurst Park and its estates were sold to the Duke of Norfolk in 1806. So if William entered Thomas Charles Medwin's service in 1776, it must have been quite soon after his arrival in Horsham, and Wiliam would have only been a boy of fourteen. But William obviously showed promise and intelligence, because he was quite

---

30   HM MSS Cat. No. 396.1
31   HM MSS Cat. No. 429.13

quickly promoted to a position of trust. Among Medwin's responsibilities as Steward of Warminghurst was the position of gamekeeper for the Manor of Pinkhurst, which lay in the parishes of Slinfold and Billingshurst. The Medwin papers contain several written or printed declarations, signed by William Ellis, Clerk of the Peace for Sussex, and dating from the 1780s, confirming that William Cooper had been appointed to deputise as a gamekeeper for the Manor of Pinkhurst by Roger Clough Esq. and Mrs. Patty Clough, the Lords of the Manor, or by Thomas Charles Medwin as their agent.[32]

We gain a clear personal impression of William Cooper from a letter among the Medwin papers written by Samuel Evers, then his clerk, in 1786.[33] It concerns an altercation between "Squire" Nathaniel Tredcroft, the leading magistrate in Horsham, and William Cooper, who is described as Medwin's servant and "huntsman". Tredcroft berated William for hunting and said that it was a piece of insolence to the neighbouring gentry that his master should keep hounds. Tredcroft obviously considered himself a representative of the older gentry in Horsham, and judged Medwin to be an upstart. He had himself been a fanatical huntsman in his youth (according to the diary of John Baker, who lived at Horsham Park in the 1770's). But in Ever's letter he is revealed as snobbish and prejudiced, as well as extremely rude, while William was commended by Evers for his cool behaviour when under attack. Evers gave a clear and concise account of the incident to Medwin, and added his own ironic comments on Squire Tredcroft's behaviour. The description of the incident clearly indicates William's intelligence and self-confidence - qualities which doubtless made him a valuable servant and a good inn-keeper.

Horsham November 13ᵗʰ 1786

Sir,

Since I wrote you in the Morning, Page has been with W(illia)m and has told him, that Mr. Treadcroft has declar'd that he will take every Opportunity to lodge an Information against him, which its (sic) at present out of his Power to do, as W(illia)m says that he did not see them kill any thing, and y t (that) Page was not seen by him Yesterday - however W(illia)m thinks he has it in his power to return Treadcroft's civility, as his Man who hunts the Hounds has no Deputation, nor has his Master taken out any Licence for him[34] and he is determined to Watch both Cragg and him, and lodge an Information agsᵗ (against) them provided you have no objection - I cannot help observing that Treadcroft's behaviour has been very Unbecoming the character of a Gentleman, for I think no person in that Station wou'd have been so mean as to have told a Gentleman's Servant that "his Master had no Authority to keep Hounds, and that he wou'd no suffer him to do it, as it was a great piece of Insolence towards the Neighbouring Gentry". *I am happy to add that W(illia)m's deportment was Strictly consistent, and altho' T gave him very gross Language and descended so low as to abuse him - he did not give him any saucy answers but coolly Argued with him on the Impropriety of his conduct.*

I am Sir, Your most H(umbl)e servant, Sam. Evers

It is interesting that a draft of Medwin's letter to Tredcroft has also survived.[35] This reveals a much greater degree of social anxiety on Medwin's part concerning this incident. Medwin showed no sign of taking up William's suggestion that he should take the war to the enemy's camp, by collecting enough evidence to lodge a complaint against Tredcroft because his huntsman had no official deputation as a gamekeeper. Though Medwin asserted his right to keep hounds, he did not venture to reprove Tredcroft for his rudeness towards himself and his servant, but expressed his willingness to call upon him and discuss the matter *"with Temper and as a gentleman",* and said that he did not wish to be at odds with any of the neighbouring gentry.

Another letter has survived from William Cooper himself, to Medwin, giving him happy news of the birth of his fourth son Henry (the Medwins had lost their first son, Charles, in infancy, so Thomas Charles

---

[32] HM MSS Cat. Nos. 545.8, 9, 12 and 14.
[33] HM MSS Cat. No. 545.1
[34] The game laws at this time were very strict, and required a licence or a "deputation" as gamekeeper from a landowner to allow the hunting of game.
[35] HM MSS Cat. No. 545.2

would have been anxious to know if the new baby was likely to survive).[36] In a short note dated 10 February 1790, and addressed to Thomas Charles Medwin at the White Horse Inn, Fetter Lane, in London, William said simply that he was writing on behalf of Mr. Burry[37] to say that Mrs. Medwin had given birth to *"a fine boy this morning"*. William was thus clearly literate and trusted by the Medwins and Dr. Burry to relay important news.   Other papers concerning William Cooper in the Horsham Museum archives are HM MSS Cat. No. 386, a civil case brought by Henry Cock versus William Cooper, concerning property in Cowfold, before the Court of King's Bench in 1800. William had apparently bought Park Gate Farm in Cowfold from a Richard Cock, who was probably from another branch of the same family as his mother.   Richard's uncle Henry disputed his right to sell the farm. (This case has not been extracted for this Appendix because it deals far more with the quarrels between the Cocks than with William Cooper, who is really only mentioned in passing).

The most important case in which William was concerned is covered by a large bundle of documents (HM MSS Cat. No. 412), of which an edited summary has been prepared by John Hurd.   This was a case against Benjamin Boorer, who unsuccessfully contested the will of John Boorer, for leaving his farms in Warnham to William Cooper, who had been his friend as well as his tenant. A large number of witnesses testified to William Cooper's care and concern for John Boorer, when drunk, and this had persuaded John to leave his property to William Cooper, rather than his uncle Benjamin, who was known to be a wastrel. Following on from this is HM MSS Cat. No. 417, the criminal case brought by William Cooper against Dendy Napper for assault (which is included in Chapter One). There is mention in this case of the civil action against Boorer in which Cooper had just been involved.   Dendy Napper was clearly a friend of Benjamin Boorer and took his side of the dispute, to such an extent that Napper actually beat up William Cooper quite severely in a public house in Warnham, when drunk.

There are also civil cases, one involving debts to a brewer, in 1805, and others relating to William Cooper's affairs after his death, fought by Thomas Charles Medwin on his behalf, as his executor.   HM MSS Cat. No 418 is a case between the executors of Thomas Cooper, late of Leatherhead, common brewer, versus William Cooper of Horsham, inn-holder, for debt, King's Bench, 1805. This contains the brief for William Cooper's defence.   HM MSS Cat. No. 429 concerns a Chancery case brought by Edmund Glynn - who had by now married William Cooper's widow, Jane - against Thomas Charles Medwin and the other trustees and executors of William Cooper, late of Warnham and Horsham, innholder, deceased, in Chancery, 1809-1812. The papers for the defence, 2 bundles, include inventories, dated 1806, of the *Green Dragon* in Horsham, and of Thatchers and Hills Farms in Warnham, and other papers going back to 1784.   They have been summarised, but not extracted in detail, and contain a long list of bills appertaining to the estate. Surprisingly enough, William's widow Jane, who died on 29 March 1814, is apparently buried with him, according to the trancription of the tombstone, even though she married Edmund Glynn, who fought the Chancery case against William Cooper's executors.

HM MSS Cat. No. 412 (19 docs)   - *edited summary by John Hurd*

Benjamin Boorer of Warnham vs William Cooper innholder of the Green Dragon Horsham, concerning the estate of John Boorer of Warnham yeoman deceased.

Horsham Assizes, 19th March 1804

The case for the defence

John Boorer senior died in 1767 leaving estates in Wescott, Allberry, Shalford and Shere in Surrey to his son **Benjamin Boorer** (the plaintiff).[38] John Boorer left 60 acres in Warnham to his son **Robert** who died intestate leaving a son, **John Boorer,** junior, aged about 9, in the guardianship of his uncle Benjamin.[39] It was reported that Benjamin had soon dissipated his inheritance and had been reduced almost to the state of a common labourer.   John Boorer junior did not marry; he had no brothers or sisters. It is clear that

---

[36]   HM MSS Cat. No. 543.81, dated 10 February 1790.
[37]   John Burry was a surgeon and accoucheur who lived in West Street.
[38]   Benjamin Boorer was born in 1741, the youngest of six children of John and Elizabeth Boorer of Warnham.
[39]   John Boorer was born in 1766, the only son of Robert and Sarah Boorer.

his uncle Benjamin expected that the land in Warnham and another house and land at Rusper would remain in the family and that his children **Benjamin**, **William** and **Elizabeth** would inherit. However, the relationship between Benjamin and nephew John was not good: both appear to have been strong-minded people given to bouts of hard drinking. John believed that his uncle, having wasted his own inheritance, was attempting to dissipate his. It appears that the Warnham lands were encumbered by a payment of £500 to Benjamin: John stated that this had been paid but no proof of discharge had been given. Numerous witnesses testified to John Boorer's character and conduct. The consensus was that he was given to occasional bouts of severe drunkenness but when he was sober, often for several months, he was an intelligent, hardworking man. He sometimes worked at husbandry but he was a keen sportsman and acted as gamekeeper to a neighbouring gentleman. For years he served as a juryman at Horsham Midsummer Assizes.

William Cooper (the defendant) had been landlord of the *Green Dragon* in Horsham for about 13 years and had previously been a servant with Mr Medwin for about 15 years. Soon after taking the inn Cooper became acquainted with John Boorer and in 1796 took a 21-year lease on the farm at Warnham (which was called Thatchers and Hills). The farm was in a poor state and in 1801 John Boorer arranged to borrow £300 to £400 to enable Cooper to manure and cultivate the land, and to erect a new private brewhouse. It was also agreed that John Boorer was to receive a life annuity of £30. Medwin asked to see the deeds but was told that these were in the hands of uncle Benjamin and John did not like to ask him for them: Medwin arranged the mortgage without seeing the deeds. It is clear that Boorer sometimes received part of his annuity in kind at the *Green Dragon*, and also arranged for Cooper to purchase food and clothing on his behalf.

Quite often Boorer would arrive at the *Green Dragon* already the worse for drink and on these occasions Cooper prevented others from taking advantage of him and often refused to serve him liquor. **John Pledge** was a waiter at the *Green Dragon* and had frequently been told to put water and tea into gin instead of brandy to keep John Boorer from being intoxicated. **Robert Eason** boarded at the *Green Dragon* for some years and often heard Cooper deny Boorer liquor when he had been intoxicated and had often sobered him and then taken him to Warnham. **Edward Briggs** gave similar testimony, as did **William Searle** who boarded at the *Green Dragon* between 1791 and 1797. They agreed that Boorer always spoke affectionately of William Cooper who was like a brother to him.

Many people heard Boorer say that he would make Cooper his heir. **James Robertson** (clerk to Mr. Medwin) lodged at Cooper's house in 1795 and remembered that he heard Boorer say that Cooper had often cared for him and he liked *"Little Willy"* better than anybody in the world. **Nathan Blake** had similar recollections. **Daniel Owen**, aged about 13 or 14, son of **James Owen** of Warnham, lived next door to John Boorer; he remembered going shooting with **Allen Etheridge** and John Boorer in 1802 and that John Boorer said that he was minded to let Cooper have the farm when he died; he also remembered him saying that the uncle was a bad man who did not use him well. **James Figg** had known Boorer 20 years; **Stephen Pledge** had known John Boorer for 3 years; they and **Martha Pledge** and **William Chapman** of Warnham often heard Boorer speak well of Cooper and abuse his uncle. **Elizabeth March** of *The Compasses* at Rowhook gave similar testimony. **William Charman** of *The Crab Tree* at Beeding many times heard Boorer declare when sober that Cooper was an excellent tenant for whom he had a great respect and with whom he felt at home.

John Boorer's readiness to denigrate his uncle and to speak well of Cooper led people to speculate and to take sides in the matter of the future inheritance. In 1802, **Henry Groombridge**, carpenter, was employed by John Boorer to do repairs at his farm at Rusper. Boorer assisted him digging post-holes and putting up a new hog pound. Groombridge told him that people were saying that Cooper wanted to get his estate to which Boorer relied that Cooper was the best friend he ever had. Groombridge said that he should leave his property to his relations to which Boore replied, *"It's nothing to anybody who I choose to give it to, but if I continue in the mind I am now my uncle shall never have it as he has spent enough of his own and shall never spend mine!"* He said that he had no father, mother, brother or sister - but if he had a brother he could not like him better than he did Cooper who would often get him out of trouble.

Charles Ansell had known Cooper for more than 20 years; they went to school together. He claimed that Boorer and he were cutting stubble together when Boorer complained that he had difficulty getting his money from Cooper. **Stephen Pledge** countered this by saying that Boorer never cut stubble or used a scythe in his life, he was a gamekeeper to **Mr Budgen**. Ansell agreed that Boorer told him that Cooper had paid. **John Osmer, Jane Martin** of the *Dog and Bacon*, **Samuel Chatfield** and **William Steer** each recollected occasions when Boorer denigrated Cooper. **William Tasker** referred to an occasion when Cooper was in London and John Boorer expressed anxiety that he would lose his rents and borrowed £5 to put the bailiffs in. However, it has been established that Tasker told Boorer that Cooper was broke and had absconded and that he had forced the £5 on Boorer and urged him to employ bailiffs. **Mary Jeal** claimed that she had assisted Mrs Owen when John Boorer was ill - but **Mary Owen** would testify that Jeal did not assist at that time, also that Jeal was a woman of very bad character and that Mary Owen and Martha Pledge would not believe her, even on her oath; she is niece by marriage of Benjamin Boorer. **Nicholas Goodjer** said that, on 18th or 19th August 1803, he met John Boorer near the *Dog and Bacon* and that they spoke about making wills. Goodjer said that Boorer said *"The Coopers are a bad family - I mean to take care of my relations and young Ben shall have it."* (It was put to Goodjer that he must have got the date wrong, because from July 18th until his death, Boorer was ill and confined to his bed and incapable of going to Horsham).

On Wednesday 28th July 1802 John Boorer and his uncle Benjamin had been drinking at Cooper's house; Cooper was not present because he had business in London until the Saturday. During Cooper's absence John Boorer was kept continually drunk by his uncle and was taken to **Mr Sandham**, an Attorney in Horsham, to give instructions concerning his will. They returned on the Saturday but did not execute the will until the 2nd August with **John Agate** and **John Ireland**, farmers of Warnham. At the same time a Power of Attorney was executed in favour of Benjamin, authorising him to receive John Boorer's rents, settle accounts and to act generally in all his affairs. It was remarked however that the uncle never settled any account with Cooper or any other person.

A drunk man by Walter Geikie (1830)

Henry Groombridge was working at the *Lamb Inn*, Horsham. He saw John Boorer, Benjamin Boorer; John Agate and John Ireland going into the *Lamb Inn*. John Boorer was drunk and not half-an-hour later was carried to bed by **Edward** and **John Aldridge**; Agate and Ireland left but the uncle remained. **John Pledge** saw John Boorer, Agate and Ireland go into the house of Mr Sandham, the attorney, in West Street Horsham; John Boorer was very drunk. Groombridge spoke with John Boorer about 3 weeks later and said, *"I heard that you gave your uncle Ben a Power of Attorney"*. Boorer smiled and said that he had been drunk and didn't know what he had been doing but he would later alter all that.

James Owen said that in August he found John Boorer drunk upstairs and his uncle Benjamin drunk and asleep on the turnip bed. The uncle pointed to his nephew and said, *"He is now nobody - he can't pay or receive anything, he is all under me and you must settle with me for your rent!"* Owen replied that he owed no rent. About 3 weeks afterwards John Boorer and Owen were walking towards Horsham; Boorer complained of his uncle's conduct on which Owen said, *"How came you to put yourself apprentice to your uncle Ben?"* Boorer replied that he was drunk and expressed anger against Mr Agate for taking him to Mr Sandham's; he also said that Ireland had no business with it. He said that if *"Old Ben"* was to have the farm, Agate and Ireland would get some of it. He said that uncle Ben had spent his own fortune and would spend his but, *"When I die they will be disappointed - I will look on him and remember him nevertheless - I should not have known what to do but for Cooper - he has often kept me sober and prevented my drinking - and my old uncle Ben is always getting what he can from me!"* He said if it had not been for Cooper he would have spent what he had long ago. In September 1802 John Boorer was taken ill at *The Queen's Head* Horsham kept by **Nathan Blake**. He was there almost a week. He asked to see Mr Medwin concerning his will.

John Boorer was ill again in March 1803 and asked **Ned Taylor** to go to Cooper at Horsham and to ask him to send for a doctor; **Mr Stephen Dendy,** surgeon and apothecary of Horsham, attended. Food and medicine were sent by Cooper until late April. John Boorer was ill for 4 or 5 weeks and when he was better he went to see Cooper at Horsham. In May Boorer was sent home from the *Lamb Inn* at Horsham where he had been drinking for several days & was quite ill. Benjamin the uncle said, *"If anything happens, you come to me and don't go to Cooper and I'll give you a good reward."* In June Boorer got extremely drunk at the *Dog and Bacon* on Horsham Common and was taken by his uncle and his daughter to the uncle's house. Mr Dendy saw him again in Horsham about 3 weeks later but he was ill soon afterwards and was confined to his room for about a month. Stephen Dendy again attended John Boorer at the house of James Owen at Warnham late in 1803. He prescribed medicine which was sent by Cooper. Dendy met Boorer several times at Warnham, Kingsfold and Horsham Common and attended him at Owen's between 23rd and 28th June 1803. In July 1803, just before Horsham Fair, he saw Boorer at Cooper's house, he was not intoxicated but weak. On 18th July, the day of Horsham Fair, Benjamin Boorer came to inform him that John Boorer was very ill; he prescribed medicine. Dendy said that he had often warned Boorer concerning his drinking. In his opinion, based on several conversations at Owen's house and in his uncle's house and at other times, Boorer exhibited not the smallest defect of understanding but, on the contrary, appeared to possess a strong mind and an obstinate or self-willed temper. Dendy considered that it was not in the power of any person to persuade John Boorer to do any act contrary to his own inclination.

James Owen recollected that during Boorer's last illness **John Mitchell** (whose mother was sister to Benjamin Boorer's wife) had been to shave John Boorer; he said, *"Damn him, we shall have him this heat safe enough!"* Owen had seen John drink 10 glasses of wine, gin and beer. About 2 or 3 days before he died bedclothes were taken from the house by Benjamin and, on the morning of his death, the uncle took a box in which John usually kept his money and papers. John Boorer died on the 24th August, 1803. On the 27th August, the day of the funeral, James Robertson (Medwin's clerk) was sent to Warnham to ask whether John Boorer had made any subsequent will and spoke to John Ireland and Benjamin Boorer, who informed him that that he was the heir and that Cooper was not. It was thought proper to retain counsel on behalf of Cooper and on the 30th Mr Medwin gave Benjamin Boorer an attested copy of the will of 8th September. On the 24th (?September), **John Medwin** (eldest son of Thomas Charles) and James

Robertson went to Warnham to tender £15, being three-quarters of the annuity due to Benjamin Boorer; they found him working in a field belonging to John Ireland. Boorer refused the money and refused to sign a release as required by the the will of John Boorer dated 1800. Boorer repeated *"I'll have none of your money - you may go the hell together!"* John Medwin laid the notice on the ground.

On the 18th January 1804 Cooper was served with a demand for rent and arrears of Thatchers and Hills in Warnham, being £72 which Benjamin Boorer demanded as *"heir at Law."*[40] Thatchers and Hills were part of the Manor of Warnham. The manorial Court attempted to determine the rightful heir but in 1806 counsel's opinion was that the Court was not competent to decide because it had not seen John Boorer's valid will. The Court could, in the circumstances, only declare that the tenant had died and then wait to see who would claim admission to the properties.

John Boorer made three wills reflecting his deteriorating relationship with his uncle Benjamin. In a will dated 1795 he bequeathed his uncle Benjamin £20 annuity for life; Benjamin's children were to receive £100 each. In a will dated 1800 he made the same bequests but the annuity was given on condition that Benjamin would release the estate from a sum of £500 charged by the will of **John Boorer** the grandfather of John; the £500 had been paid but no discharge had been given. In his last will dated 8th September 1802, John Boorer removed the legacies to Benjamin Boorer's children: the sole beneficiary and executor was to be **William Cooper,** innholder of the Green Dragon Horsham. This will was witnessed by James Robertson (clerk to Thomas Charles Medwin) and Nathan Blake of the *Queen's Head Inn*, Horsham. Apparently, **Stephen Harding** was to be called to give evidence for the prosecution that Boorer was drunk when he went to Medwin to make his will. This was to be countered by information that Harding was heard to say that he wanted revenge because Cooper had cut off an entail of Dick's Farm at Cowfold which he, Harding, would have had if his wife had lived.

There was good reason to believe that the court action would never have commenced but for the animosity against Cooper on the part of **Mr. Dendy Napper** of Warnham. Napper and Cooper had been friends but Napper had gained an unsatisfactory verdict in a case concerning himself and Cooper over a right to cut timber. *(There are no papers relating to this case in Horsham Museum).* Napper was heard to say *"I'll work him - it shan't stand still for want of money; I'll spend* Old House Farm *but what I'll have revenge of Cooper!"* Napper was a Warnham Parish Officer and was reported as going to several poor persons who were to be witnesses in the Boorer-Cooper case and telling them that none of them should have any Parish Relief.

HM MSS Cat. No. 418 - *extracted by* **John Hurd**

Horsham Assizes 23 Mar 1805 (*note:* Lewes Assizes 1805 refreshor)

William Cooper against **Mr Coffin** and **Mr Florance Young (executors of Thomas Cooper)**

Thomas Cooper a common brewer of Leatherhead died 17th July 1800. His Executors claimed that **William Cooper** of the *Green Dragon,* Horsham, owed £351.6s.6d for beer and other supplies - also, despite repeated requests for payment and William Cooper's promises, he continued *"fraudulently intending craftily and subtly to deceive and defraud"* Thomas Cooper's estate. William Cooper countered by saying that Thomas's estate owed him £500 for goods supplied. He also said that he had been over-charged for beer and that he had not been given the usual allowance for *"Butt Money"* or for a quantity of clover seeds. He had not seen detailed accounts. He could prove that some of the money had been paid to the estate - chiefly noting a Bond for £100 for which he had the receipt of **Florance Young** and a Bill of Exchange for £100 drawn on the Horsham Bank on Wilkinson, Bloxam & Co., which was paid to the estate's attorney, Mr Pryne. The Bill of Exchange was endorsed *"for the Executors of T. Cooper"* and had been cashed and bore the signatures of **Messrs Pryne** and **Coffin** - and was in the possession of William Cooper, who regarded these as firm evidence of poor accounting.

---

40 "Heir at law" was the closest known relation.

On 19th November 1803 William Cooper was arrested on the affidavit of Mr Coffin. He had suddenly to procure Special Bail before a Commission 20 miles from his home and lost expenses of £10 in taking his bail to Brighthelmstone and then *"perfecting the same"* in London. On remonstrating with Mr Pryne that Coffin's claim which formed the basis for his affadavit was at least £100 more than could possibly be due, Mr Pryne first excused himself saying *"There was a mistake!"* Medwin suggested that his own and his client's *"difficulties"* led him to discontinue the action in Hilary Term on payment of costs, and on 8th February 1804 brought a fresh action. A balance sheet indicated that £149.2.6d was due - William Cooper submitted accounts to show that he was owed £51.13.6d.

In Chancery Between Edmund Glynn & Jane his wife William Cooper Jas Cooper Sarah Cooper & Nathan Cooper Infants by Edwd Glynn their next frd ——— Plts

Thomas Charles Medwin Stepn Dendy and Richard Thornton & Thomas Cooper an Infant by James Bayley his Guardian ——————— Defts

An Inventory of the Household furniture and other Effects of the Testator Willm. Cooper in the Pleadings of this Cause named at the Green Dragon Inn in Horsham in the County of Sussex the use where of is given by the said Testor's Will to the said Plt Jane Glynn for her Life ——

Kitchen ... One Range One Crane two pothooks —— One poker one small smoke Jack 2 Spits and holdfast & Iron Candlesticks Copper kitchen &c Coal Scuttles Do

Horsham Museum MSS Cat. No. 429.29. Inventory of the Green Dragon Inn, Bishopric
(first page of six)

Edmund Glyn and Jane his wife (late Cooper) and others   vs   **Thomas Charles Medwin, Stephen Dendy and Richard Thornton** *(trustees of the late William Cooper)* **and Thomas Cooper, infant, concerning the will of William Cooper, dated 18ᵗʰ November, 1805.**

In Chancery

The case for the defence

William Cooper's property included Thatcher's and Hills farms in Warnham and the *Green Dragon Inn* in the Bishopric, Horsham. **Thomas Charles Medwin**, (lawyer), **Stephen Dendy** (surgeon) and **Richard Thornton** (brewer) were made his trustees and charged to sell all his property for the maintenance of his children, but they were directed that his wife should be allowed to carry on his business at the *Green Dragon Inn.* In a codicil, he left the *Dog and Bacon Inn* to the use of Richard Thornton. **Edmund Glynn** has now married **Jane Cooper** née Fiest (widow of William) and is running the *Green Dragon.* The Glynns claim that the defendants have not sold the farm as directed by the will and now say that only the furniture and goods of the *Green Dragon* must be sold to pay the debts on the estate. The farm has been let for £50 per annum to Richard Grinsted *(a partner in the Horsham Bank run by John Lanham and Charles Grinsted - brother of Richard).* The defendants say that renting the farm has been more beneficial to the children than selling it, and deny that they have refused to give accounts. Thomas Cooper has been placed as an apprentice to **James Killick o**f Dorking, and they have paid an annuity due to **Benjamin Boorer** on the Warnham property. Thomas Charles Medwin claims that he is owed several sums by the estate.

The first schedule attached is an inventory of the *Green Dragon Inn* and the farms in Warnham, the second and third schedules give accounts of the monies paid and received, and the fourth schedule gives details of bonds and annuities owned by William Cooper. Depositions of witnesses are also attached, dated 20ᵗʰ and 21ˢᵗ September 1808, with occupations and ages of **James Robertson** (clerk to Thomas Charles Medwin, gent., aged 43), **Nathan Blake** (victualler, aged 33), **Robert Eason** (china man, aged 48) , **John Agate** (carpenter, aged 41), **William Joanes** (surveyor, aged 40), **Robert Wood** (farmer, aged 39), **Robert Boreman** (farmer, aged 54) , **Samuel Fiest** (brother of Jane Cooper, now Glynn, aged 44) and **Richard Grinsted, (**gent., aged 32). The inventory and appraisement of the effects at the Warnham farms - Thatcher's and Hills Farms - livestock and farming equipment worth £721.19s.9d - and Chicken and Slaughter Bridge Farm - livestock and farming equipment worth £270.10s.9d; gives a total of £992.10s.6d. The inventory of household furniture and stock in trade of the *Green Dragon Inn,* valued by **Drew Michell** and **W. Chambers**, amounted to £345.13s.9d for the furniture and £150 for drink. There is an original copy of the will of William Cooper, dated 10 November 1805, for which probate was granted on 9ᵗʰ June 1806. A codicil drafted in 1805 concerned the purchase of the *Dog and Bacon Inn*, for which William Cooper was the best bidder, but apparently he had agreed to purchase it for Richard Thornton. *(There is some evidence to suggest that this Richard Thornton, eldest son of the schoolmaster, was not very bright - or more probably had learning difficulties - so it is not surprising that he needed William Cooper's help to transact a property deal).* The codicil directs Cooper's executors to complete the purchase and Richard Thornton to pay £860 for the property.

A later brief for the defendants, to support the Master's report, quotes the judgements of 17ᵗʰ February 1809 and 26ᵗʰ January 1811 in full, plus exceptions to the report. There are annotated copies of the affidavits sworn by William Joanes, John Agate, Stephen Dendy, Richard Thornton and James Robertson, relating to the Boorer annuity. This involved **Philip Chasemore**, butcher and (cattle) salesman, who was paid £300 in settlement. Finally, a brief for **Thomas Cooper**, infant, (dated ?1811) mentions the 1809 and 1811 judgements, detailing further investigations and measures taken to determine the above case and resolve the question of the Boorer annuity. Eventually it seems to have been concluded that the defendants had not misused the money, and Nathan Blake was appointed as guardian of the children.

One thing that emerges from these documents is that William Cooper was deeply involved in the Horsham Friendly Society, instituted on 7 July 1794 with 88 members, and by 1796 *"lately established at the house of the said William Cooper known by the sign of the Green Dragon"* . In this same year, William Cooper was appointed Treasurer, and had a *"chest or box"* deposited at his house for safe keeping, containing papers, money and securities.   A bond was signed on 6 June 1796 by **William Cooper, Charles Linfield** *(of Coolhurst)* and **William Nye**, gent., for £200 to be held in trust for the Society. Presumably this money was intended by the Friendly Society to be used for the benefit of its members, as an insurance against sickness and unemployment, in a way which foreshadowed the welfare state.   By 1800, William Cooper was asked to transfer the stock he held to **William Murrell**, the new Treasurer - presumably the £200 3% stock he had held under the 1796 Bond - and he received a receipt for a year and a half's dividend - £9. Other people associated with the Friendly Society at this time were **John Bates**, **Henry Harding, John Manvell** and **Thomas Honeywood** as Steward, and Cooper's papers include a copy of the Society's rules.

These two bundles of papers (containing more than 50 documents) also contain a great number of bills on the estate of William Cooper, mainly relating to bricklaying and carpentry work done on the Warnham farms and the stock in trade of the *Green Dragon*, from 1795 to 1807.   Among these are included a bill from Henry Charman of £10.15s. for board and lodgings for the late Mrs. Cooper (mother of William) from 1795 to 1800 *"so that she should not live in the poor house"*.   There is also a bill for £8.7s.8⅛d for the education of sons William and James from Robert Eason, and a loan of £100 from Nathan Blake in 1805, with interest to be paid at the Horsham Bank.

There are also a number of bills from William Cooper to Thomas Charles Medwin for a wide range of services, which show how much Medwin depended upon Cooper, and how closely they worked together. These include bills in 1795 and 1796 for beer, bread and cheese, grinding malt, etc. totalling £24.18s.1d, plus 5s. for servants at the rent feast; bills in July 1802 for election work done on Medwin's behalf and a loan to his son John Medwin, totalling £36.3s.2⅛d; and bills in 1805 for farm work, horse hire and payment of wages, plus the supply of game - a brace of partridges, a pheasant and a hare - to John Medwin; no total.

There are other bills from;
John Agate (as collector of the Land Tax),
Richard Bourn, surveyor of highways in Warnham (Highway tax),
John Burrage (cooperage and the supply of beer, cider and spirits)
Charles Brooker (goods delivered)
Charles Child (for repairs at farms and carpentry work)
Joseph Holmes (repairs of metal goods)
James Howes (wines and spirits and carriage)
William Morgan ("clearing wottels")
G. Nye (bricklaying at Thatchers and Hill Farm)
William Parkhurst (carriage of goods to and from London)
Daniel Sharp (oats)
Richard Thornton (barrels and hops).

Editorial comment; these give useful information about tradesmen in Horsham at this time, and indicate those with whom William Cooper chose to deal. It is from such apparently trifling details in these bundles of papers that it is possible to build up a much larger picture of William Cooper's life, and the Horsham in which he lived.

Coopers making barrels - W.H. Pyne *(Microcosm)*

Index

This index lists nearly 400 people who are mentioned in the cases as defendants, prosecutors, witnesses, magistrates or arresting officers, or of whom there is a significant mention. In some places the information in the case has been supplemented by reference to the Land Tax or other documents - additional information added to the index has been placed in brackets. If the information is somewhat doubtful or unclear, it is preceded by a question mark.

Surname	First name	Occupation	Place	Cat	Chapter	Date
Agate,	John	farmer	Warnham	412	Appendix	1804
Agate,	Mr. John	farmer	Warnham	412	Appendix	1804
Agate,	John	carpenter	Warnham	419	Appendix	1809-1812
Agate,	Mr. (John)	farmer	Warnham	417	Chapter 1	1805
Agate,	Mr. Henry	farmer	Storrington	505	Chapter 9	1840
Akehurst,	Mary	charwoman to Mr. Baker	Cowfold	509	Chapter 12	1845
Aldridge	Mr. John	magistrate and M.P.	Horsham/Beeding	425	Chapter 12	1808
Aldridge,	Mr. (Robert)	magistrate	Horsham/Beeding	507	Chapter 12	1841
Aldridge,	Mr. (Robert)	magistrate	Horsham/Beeding	493	Chapter 12	1834
Aldridge,	Mr. Robert	magistrate	Lower Beeding	506	Chapter 12	1840
Aldridge,	Mr. (John)	magistrate and M.P.	Horsham	348	Chapter 2	1789
Aldridge,	Mr. John	magistrate and M.P.	Horsham	343	Chapter 7	1788
Aldridge,	Mr. John	magistrate and M.P.	Horsham	319	Chapter 9	1783
Ansell,	Charles	(butcher)	Horsham	412	Appendix	1804
Ansell,	Thomas junior	tanner	Horsham	319	Chapter 1	1783
Ansell,	Thomas junior	tanner	Horsham	417	Chapter 1	1805
Ansell,	Thomas senior	miller and carrier	Horsham	319	Chapter 9	1783
Ashdowne,	The Rev. Robert	Minister of Baptist Church	Horsham	524	Chapter 6	1851
Bacon,	Benjamin	constable	Southweald, Essex	506	Chapter 12	1840
Bailey,	Edward	-	?Steyning	375	Chapter 12	1796
Baines,	Mr. Thomas	stood bail for George Langley	?Washington	505	Chapter 9	1840
Baker,	Esther	servant girl	Horsham	493	Chapter 12	1834
Baker,	Richard Grey	bailiff (Lower Bewbush)	Lower Beeding	506	Chapter 12	1840
Baker,	Mr. Richard	farmer	Cowfold	509	Chapter 12	1845
Bartley,	Stanford	landlord (Black Swan)	Pease Pottage	506	Chapter 12	1840
Bates,	John	(farmer - Southwater)	Horsham	419	Appendix	1809-1812
Baytupp,	Martha	servant to Mr. John Pollard	Horsham	319	Chapter 9	1783
Belchambers,	George	-	Billingshurst	509	Chapter 12	1845
Best,	Charles	-	Steyning	348	Chapter 2	1789
Blake,	Nathan	iinkeeper (Queen's Head)	Horsham	412	Appendix	1804
Blake,	Nathan	innkeeper (Queen's Head)	Horsham	419	Appendix	1809-1812
Boghurst,	Mr.	magistrate	Worthing	505	Chapter 9	1840
Booker,	James	stable boy	Horsham	507	Chapter 12	1841
Boorer,	William	son of Benjamin Boorer	Warnham	412	Appendix	1804
Boorer,	Benjamin	farmer	Warnham	412	Appendix	1804
Boorer,	Elizabeth	daughter of Benjamin Boorer	Warnham	412	Appendix	1804
Boorer,	Benjamin	son of Benjamin Boorer	Warnham	412	Appendix	1804
Boorer,	John senior	farmer	Warnham	412	Appendix	1804
Boorer,	John junior	farmer	Warnham	412	Appendix	1804
Boorer,	Benjamin	farmer	Warnham	412	Appendix	1804
Boorer,	Benjamin	farmer	Warnham	417	Chapter 1	1805
Boreman,	Robert	farmer	?Horsham	419	Appendix	1809-1812
Botting,	Mrs. Elizabeth,	farmer's wife	Washington	375	Chapter 12	1796
Botting,	John	farmer	Washington	375	Chapter 12	1796
Bourn,	Richard	surveyor of highways	Warnham	419	Appendix	1809-1812
Bourne,	Mr. Thomas	surgeon	Horsham	510	Chapter 1	1845
Bourne,	Mrs. Elizabeth	housewife	Horsham	364	Chapter 1	1794
Bourne,	Jonathan	?constable	Nuthurst	319	Chapter 9	1783
Boxall,	Mr. and Mrs.	innkeepers	Kirdford	360	Chapter 1	1792
Boxall,	John	lath cleaver	?Pulborough	385	Chapter 12	1800
Brading,	George	-	?Washington	505	Chapter 9	1840
Briggs,	Edward	-	Horsham	412	Appendix	1804
Brooke,	Mr. George	farmer (Chesworth)	Horsham	394	Chapter 12	1801
Brooker,	Charles	-	?Horsham	419	Appendix	1809-1812
Bryant,	Mr.	lawyer	Reigate	336	Chapter 10	1787
Budgen,	Mr.	-	?Horsham	412	Appendix	1804
Burberry,	Elizabeth	landlady	Ifield Green	506	Chapter 12	1840

Burdfield,	Mary	widow	Cowfold	509	Chapter 12	1845
Burrage,	John	cooper	Horsham	419	Appendix	1809-1812
Byass,	Mr. (George)	surgeon	Storrington	456	Chapter 6	1819
Caven,	Peter	constable	Horsham	343	Chapter 7	1788
Chambers,	William	(innkeeper, Roughey)	Horsham	419	Appendix	1809-1812
Chapman,	William	--	Warnham	412	Appendix	1804
Chapman,	James jun.	?labourer	?Rusper	354	Chapter 1	1790
Charlwood,	Timothy	ostler at King's Head, Tooting	London	506	Chapter 12	1840
Charman,	William	innkeeper (Crab Tree)	(Lower) Beeding	412	Appendix	1804
Charman,	Henry	(farmer)	Warnham	419	Appendix	1809-1812
Charman,	George senior	postboy at the King's Head Inn	Horsham	508	Chapter 12	1843
Charman,	George junior	boy	Horsham	508	Chapter 12	1843
Charman,	Sarah	housekeeper (Anchor Tap)	Horsham	504	Chapter 8	1840
Charman,	Richard	innkeeper (Anchor Tap)	Horsham	504	Chapter 8	1840
Charman,	Henry	postboy	Horsham	504	Chapter 8	1840
Charman,	Ian	-	?Washington	505	Chapter 9	1840
Chasemore,	Mr. Philip	butcher, salesman	Horsham	419	Appendix	1809-1812
Chasemore,	Mr. Philip	farmer	Horsham	492	Chapter 12	1833
Chatfield,	Samuel	-	Horsham	412	Appendix	1804
Chatfield,	Mr. John	landowner	Thakeham Place	385	Chapter 12	1800
Chatfield,	John	-	Horsham	639	Chapter 6	1830
Cheeseman,	George	ostler	Horsham	504	Chapter 8	1840
Child,	Charles	carpenter	Warnham	419	Appendix	1809-1812
Clark,	Thomas	friend of John Hughes	?Rye	435	Chapter 3	1812
Coffin	Mr.	executor of Thomas Cooper	?Leatherhead	418	Appendix	1805
Coleman,	Dr. (William Thomas)	former master of James Sadler	Horsham	507	Chapter 12	1841
Coles,	Thomas	tramp	(no fixed abode)	509	Chapter 12	1845
Collett,	Jeremiah	baker	Horsham	510	Chapter 1	1845
Cooper,	William (late)	innkeeper (Green Dragon)	Horsham	419	Appendix	1809-1812
Cooper,	William	innkeeper (Green Dragon)	Horsham	418	Appendix	1805
Cooper,	Thomas	brewer	Leatherhead	418	Appendix	1805
Cooper,	William	innkeeper, formerly Medwins' servant	Horsham	412	Appendix	1804
Cooper,	William (late)	innkeeper and farmer	Horsham/Warnham	429	Appendix	1809-1812
Cooper,	William	innkeeper and farmer	Horsham/Warnham	418	Appendix	1805
Cooper,	Thomas	son of William Cooper	Horsham	419	Appendix	1809-1812
Cooper,	Mrs. (late)	mother of William Cooper	Horsham	419	Appendix	1809-1812
Cooper,	William	innkeeper and farmer	Horsham/Warnham	412	Appendix	1804
Cooper,	William	innkeeper and farmer	Horsham/Warnham	360	Chapter 1	1792
Cooper,	Frances	child	Horsham	364	Chapter 1	1794
Cooper,	William	innkeeper and farmer	Horsham/Warnham	417	Chapter 1	1805
Cooper,	Abraham	?labourer	Wisborough Green	360	Chapter 1	1792
Cuckney,	John	higler	Steyning	375	Chapter 12	1796
Dale,	James	labourer	Horsham	492	Chapter 12	1833
Dendy,	Mr. Stephen	apothecary (and surgeon)	Horsham	412	Appendix	1804
Dendy,	Mr. Stephen	surgeon, executor and trustee	Horsham	419	Appendix	1809-1812
Dendy,	Thomas	corn chandler	Horsham	422	Chapter 4	1806
Dendy,	Cassandra	kept chandler's shop	Horsham	422	Chapter 4	1806
Dendy,	Peter	farmer	Itchingfield	452	Chapter 5	1818
Dendy,	Thomas	baker	Horsham	524	Chapter 6	1851
Denman,	Thomas	labourer	?Ifield	506	Chapter 12	1840
Dennett,	Mr. (Thomas)	surgeon	Storrington	456	Chapter 6	1819
Draper,	Mrs. Elizabeth	widow of Captain Draper	Horsham	343	Chapter 7	1788
Drewitt,	Edmund	brother of Robert Drewitt	?Midhurst	304	Chapter 12	1777
Drewitt,	Robert	servant to exciseman Gray	?Midhurst	304	Chapter 12	1777
Durrant,	William	labourer	Horsham	452	Chapter 5	1818
Eason,	Robert	china man (merchant), tutor	Horsham	419	Appendix	1809-1812
Eason,	Robert	china man (merchant)	Horsham	412	Appendix	1804
Edwards,	-	associate of the Stennings	Whitely, Surrey	348	Chapter 2	1789
Elliott,	Mr. Thomas	farmer and Land Tax collector	Wisborough Green	327	Chapter 12	1785
Ellis,	John Lutman	coroner	Chichester	456	Chapter 6	1819
Ellis,	Mr. William	lawyer and Clerk of the Peace	Horsham	343	Chapter 7	1788
Elms,	Mr. Richard	farmer and Land Tax collector	Wisborough Green	327	Chapter 12	1785
Elms,	Mrs.	lady who lived in the Causeway	Horsham	524	Chapter 6	1851
Etheridge,	Allen	(huntsman to Sir Bysshe Shelley in 1812)	Horsham	412	Appendix	1804

Etherton,	Edmund	blacksmith	Horsham	452	Chapter 5	1818
Evans,	(the Rev.) Mr.(Morgan)	(curate)	Wisborough Green	360	Chapter 1	1792
Evans,	William	-	Horsham	307	Chapter 10	1777
Evans,	The Rev. Mr. Thomas	former curate of Cuckfield	Seaford	336	Chapter 10	1787
Evans,	the Rev. Mr. Morgan	curate of Kirdford & Wisborough Green	Wisborough Green	327	Chapter 12	1785
Feist,	Samuel	brother of Jane (Cooper) Glyn	?Horsham	419	Appendix	1809-1812
Feist,	Charles	constable	Horsham	507	Chapter 12	1841
Feist,	Charles	constable	Horsham	509	Chapter 12	1845
Figg,	James	-	?Warnham	412	Appendix	1804
Flanagan,	James	constable	?Billingshurst	509	Chapter 12	1845
Flint,	Charles	?constable	Nuthurst	319	Chapter 9	1783
Floate	"Old" (father of Sarah)	farmworker	Washington	505	Chapter 9	1840
Floate,	Mrs.	mother of Sarah Floate	Washington	505	Chapter 9	1840
Floate,	Sarah	farmworker	Washington	505	Chapter 9	1840
Floate,	Mr. Henry	farmer	Washington	505	Chapter 9	1840
Fuller,	Mrs.	lady living at Warnham Court	Warnham	524	Chapter 6	1851
Garman,	Eliza	sister of Sarah Charman	Horsham	504	Chapter 8	1840
Garnier,	Louis	French prisoner	France	435	Chapter 3	1812
Garrard,	Mr.	farmer	Rusper	354	Chapter 1	1790
Gasson,	Henry	carter (Lower Bewbush)	Lower Beeding	506	Chapter 12	1840
Gates,	George	servant to Mr. Plumer	Horsham	524	Chapter 6	1851
Geere,	James	labourer	Storrington	456	Chapter 6	1819
Gibson,	John	tollgate keeper	London/Brighton road	506	Chapter 12	1840
Gibson,	William	boy	Horsham	524	Chapter 6	1851
Gibson,	Mr.	magistrate	Storrington	505	Chapter 9	1840
Gilburd,	Charles	friend of William Evans	Horsham	307	Chapter 10	1777
Glyn,	Jane (Cooper)	widow of William Cooper, remarried	Horsham	419	Appendix	1809-1812
Glyn,	Edmund	innkeeper (Green Dragon)	Horsham	419	Appendix	1809-1812
Goatcher,	Richard	thatcher	?Warminghurst	505	Chapter 9	1840
Golding,	Ann	housekeeper	Horsham/London	422	Chapter 4	1806
Goodjer,	Nicholas	(glazier)	Horsham	412	Appendix	1804
Goring,	Mr. (Charles)	magistrate	Wiston	375	Chapter 12	1796
Goring,	Mr.	landowner	Wiston	505	Chapter 9	1840
Gower	(John Coppard)	policeman	Horsham	508	Chapter 12	1843
Gower,	(John Coppard)	policeman	Horsham	509	Chapter 12	1845
Gray,	Thomas	exciseman	Holborn, London	304	Chapter 12	1777
Greenfield,	William	farmer	?Pulborough	385	Chapter 12	1800
Grinsted,	Richard	partner in Horsham Bank	Horsham	419	Appendix	1809-1812
Grinsted,	Charles	partner in Horsham Bank	Horsham	419	Appendix	1809-1812
Groombridge,	Henry	carpenter	Horsham	412	Appendix	1804
Gudgeon,	-	former servant of Mr. Padwick	Horsham	507	Chapter 12	1841
Hack,	-	policeman	Washington	505	Chapter 9	1840
Haines,	Mr. John	farmer	Wisborough Green	327	Chapter 12	1785
Haines,	George	farmer	?Washington	505	Chapter 9	1840
Hall,	Mary, junior	servant	Horsham	510	Chapter 1	1845
Hall,	Henry	-	Horsham	510	Chapter 1	1845
Hall,	Mary, senior	kept fish and fruit shop	Horsham	510	Chapter 1	1845
Hall,	Richard	kept fish and fruit shop	Horsham	510	Chapter 1	1845
Hamblin,	John	turner and poacher	Cuckfield	336	Chapter 10	1787
Hammond,	Charlwood	landowner	Pulborough	385	Chapter 12	1800
Hammond,	Mrs. Eleanor	innkeeper's wife (Lamb Inn)	Horsham	343	Chapter 7	1788
Harden,	Henry	-	Horsham	639	Chapter 6	1830
Harding,	Henry	(?farmer - Roughey)	Horsham	419	Appendix	1809-1812
Harding,	William	constable	Horsham	364	Chapter 1	1794
Harding,	Henry	-	Horsham	639	Chapter 6	1830
Hards,	William	tollgate keeper	Horsham/Crawley	506	Chapter 12	1840
Harwood,	Daniel	labourer	Horsham	452	Chapter 5	1818
Heaseman,	-	gatekeeper at Ansty tollgate	Ansty	336	Chapter 10	1787
Heath,	Henry	carrier	Horsham	493	Chapter 12	1834
Heath,	John	shoemaker	Horsham	639	Chapter 6	1830
Heath,	Henry	carrier	Horsham	504	Chapter 8	1840
Henley,	Charles	(agricultural labourer)	Horsham	508	Chapter 12	1843
Herring,	James	chemist	Horsham	504	Chapter 8	1840
Hewett,	George	brother of Henry James Hewett	Horsham	639	Chapter 6	1830
Hewett,	Mrs.	mother of George and Henry James	Horsham	639	Chapter 6	1830

Hewett,	Henry James	lived with parents in Horsham	Horsham	639	Chapter 6	1830
Hillman,	Peter	labourer	Cowfold	509	Chapter 12	1845
Hills,	Henry	relieving officer of parish workhouse	?Washington	505	Chapter 9	1840
Hodgson,	The Rev. Mr.(servant)	manservant	Horsham	524	Chapter 6	1851
Holmes,	Joseph	locksmith, gunsmith	Horsham	419	Appendix	1809-1812
Honywood,	Thomas	carpenter, Schoolwarden of Collyers (1821)	Horsham	419	Appendix	1809-1812
Honywood,	Drew	book-keeper of Horsham Coach	Horsham	493	Chapter 12	1834
Howes,	James	wine and sprit merchant	Horsham	419	Appendix	1809-1812
Howes,	Harry	innkeeper (Crown Inn)	Horsham	425	Chapter 12	1808
Hughes,	Thomas	?slater	Horsham	425	Chapter 12	1808
Hughes,	John	innkeeper	Rye	435	Chapter 3	1812
Huntley,	Henry	labourer	Horsham	492	Chapter 12	1833
Hurst,	Robert Henry Esq.	magistrate and M.P.	Horsham	510	Chapter 1	1840-45
Hurst,	Daniel	constable	Wisborough Green	327	Chapter 12	1785
Hurst.	Mr. Robert Henry	magistrate	Horsham	504	Chapter 8	1840
Hyatt,	John		Horsham	639	Chapter 6	1830
Ireland,	John	farmer	Warnham	412	Appendix	1804
Ireland,	Miss Anne	shopkeeper of West Street	Horsham	508	Chapter 12	1843
James,	Edward	brazier, innkeeper	Steyning	417	Chapter 1	1805
Jeal,	Mary		?Warnham	412	Appendix	1804
Jenkins,	Lucy	servant to Mrs. Elms	Horsham	524	Chapter 6	1851
Joanes,	William	surveyor	Horsham	419	Appendix	1809-1812
Joanes,	Edward	labourer	Horsham	343	Chapter 7	1788
Jordan,	Henry	constable	Horsham	639	Chapter 6	1830
Kaye,	Mr. John	friend of George Langley	?Washington	505	Chapter 9	1840
Kensett,	Peter	?scrapdealer	Billingshurst	509	Chapter 12	1845
Kensett,	Edwin	son of Peter Kensett	Billingshurst	509	Chapter 12	1845
Killick,	James	-	Dorking	419	Appendix	1809-1812
Killick,	Robert	-	Horsham	524	Chapter 6	1851
Kimber,	John	park keeper and game keeper	Cuckfield	336	Chapter 10	1787
Knight,	Mr.	farmer (Bourne Hill)	Horsham	417	Chapter 1	1805
Knight,	James	-	Billingshurst	348	Chapter 2	1789
Laker,	John	tailor and salesman	Billingshurst	348	Chapter 2	1789
Laker,	William	son of John Laker	Billingshurst	348	Chapter 2	1789
Lampard,	Sarah	shop assistant	Horsham	422	Chapter 4	1806
Langley,	Henry	ostler at the King's Head Inn	Horsham	508	Chapter 12	1843
Langley,	William	peace officer	?Horsham	385	Chapter 12	1800
Langley,	George	labourer	Washington	505	Chapter 9	1840
Lanham,	John	partner in Horsham Bank	Horsham	419	Appendix	1809-1812
Linfield,	Charles	farmer (Coolhurst)	Horsham	419	Appendix	1809-1812
Linfield,	Henry	?farmer	Nuthurst	319	Chapter 9	1783
Lintott,	Mr. William	wholesale grocer	Horsham	493	Chapter 12	1834
Livrer,	George	miller	Warnham	493	Chapter 12	1834
Lomas,	Thomas	coppersmith	?Billingshurst	509	Chapter 12	1845
Longhurst,	William	labourer	Horsham	452	Chapter 5	1818
Longhurst,	Ann	young girl	Washington	505	Chapter 9	1840
Lovegrove,	Dr. Joseph	surgeon	Horsham	510	Chapter 1	1845
Lovegrove,	Dr. Joseph	surgeon	Horsham	504	Chapter 8	1840
Lovegrove,	Mr. (Joseph)	surgeon	Horsham	639	Chapter 6	1830
Lovekin,	Mrs.	neighbour	Horsham	510	Chapter 1	1845
Loxley,	Henry	constable	Horsham	492	Chapter 12	1833
Man,	John	thresher on Mr. Elliott's farm	Wisborough Green	327	Chapter 12	1785
Mance,	Mr.	keeper of Petworth gaol	Petworth	510	Chapter 1	1845
Mann,	Thomas	Methodist minister	Horsham	307	Chapter 10	1777
March,	Elizabeth	innkeeper (The Compasses)	Rowhook	412	Appendix	1804
Marchant,	John	postillion	Cuckfield	336	Chapter 10	1787
Markbee,	William	farmer	Rusper	354	Chapter 1	1790
Marsh,	Sarah	child	Horsham	364	Chapter 1	1794
Martin,	Jane	innkeeper (Dog and Bacon)	Horsham	412	Appendix	1804
Mathews,	John	ostler	Horsham	504	Chapter 8	1840
Medwin	Mr. Thomas Charles	lawyer, executor and trustee	Horsham	419	Appendix	1809-1812
Medwin,	John	eldest son, clerk in his father's office	Horsham	419	Appendix	1809-1812
Medwin,	Mr. Thomas Charles	solicitor	Horsham	412	Appendix	1804
Medwin,	Mr. Pilfold	solicitor, youngest son of Thomas Charles	Horsham	509	Chapter 12	1845

Michell,	Drew	(painter, carpenter)	Horsham	419	Appendix	1809-1812
Mills,	Mrs. Sarah	housewife	Horsham	364	Chapter 1	1794
Mitchell,	John	-	?Warnham	412	Appendix	1804
Mitchell,	Mr. John	farmer (Amblehurst)	Wisborough Green	327	Chapter 12	1785
Mitchell,	Mrs.	mother of Milford Mitchell	Horsham	492	Chapter 12	1833
Mitchell,	Milford	labourer	Horsham	492	Chapter 12	1833
Mitchell,	Stephen	-	Horsham	639	Chapter 6	1830
Mitchell,	Mrs. Stephen	-	Horsham	639	Chapter 6	1830
Moase,	Richard	farmer	?West Chiltington	385	Chapter 12	1800
Money,	Captain (servant of)	manservant	?Warnham	417	Chapter 1	1805
Moon,	(James)	apprentice to Matthias Walker	Horsham	508	Chapter 12	1843
Morgan,	William	labourer	Horsham	419	Appendix	1809-1812
Morris,	Isaac	surgeon	Wisborough Green	360	Chapter 1	1792
Morris,	John Esq.	gentleman, tenant Springfield Park	Horsham/London	422	Chapter 4	1806
Moulding,	William	farm labourer	Storrington	505	Chapter 9	1840
Murrell,	William	(painter, glazier)	Horsham	419	Appendix	1809-1812
Murrell,	Henry	plumber and glazier	Horsham	425	Chapter 12	1808
Napper,	Mr. Dendy	wealthy farmer	Warnham	412	Appendix	1804
Napper,	Mr. Dendy	wealthy farmer	Warnham	417	Chapter 1	1805
Neeves,	Mr. (Benjamin)	chemist	Horsham	508	Chapter 12	1843
Nelthorpe,	Mr. James	magistrate	Horsham	509	Chapter 12	1845
Nye,	G.	bricklayer	Horsham	419	Appendix	1809-1812
Nye,	William	gentleman	Horsham	419	Appendix	1809-1812
Oakes,	George	grocer and uncle of Charles Oakes	Horsham	493	Chapter 12	1834
Oakes,	Charles	servant to Mr. William Lintott	Horsham	493	Chapter 12	1834
Oakes,	Sheppard	cousin of George	New Cross, London	493	Chapter 12	1834
Older,	John	?innkeeper	Wisborough Green	360	Chapter 1	1792
Oldfield,	Henry	convicted thief	?	304	Chapter 12	1777
Osbaldeston,	Mrs.	former tenant of Springfield Park	Horsham	422	Chapter 4	1806
Osborn,	Charles	labourer	Washington	505	Chapter 9	1840
Osmer,	John	-	?Horsham	412	Appendix	1804
Owen,	Mary	?wife of James Owen	?Warnham	412	Appendix	1804
Owen,	James	neighbour of John Boorer	Warnham	412	Appendix	1804
Owen,	James	son of James Owen	Warnham	412	Appendix	1804
Parker,	Edmund	farm labourer	Storrington	505	Chapter 9	1840
Parkhurst,	William	carrier (ran service to London)	Horsham	419	Appendix	1809-1812
Paskins,	William	-	?Steyning	375	Chapter 12	1796
Passell,	Francis	labourer	Horsham	343	Chapter 7	1788
Passell,	William	-	Horsham	504	Chapter 8	1840
Pavey (or Pacy)	Mr.	farmer	Wisborough Green	327	Chapter 12	1785
Payne,	John	boy	Horsham	524	Chapter 6	1851
Penfold,	John or James	-	Horsham	510	Chapter 1	1845
Penfold,	Henry	labourer	Horsham	394	Chapter 12	1801
Peters,	Jane	servant at Crown inn	Horsham	425	Chapter 12	1808
Philipson,	Gene	French prisoner	France	435	Chapter 3	1812
Philpot,	Thomas	worked for Nicholas Whitmore	Horsham	452	Chapter 5	1818
Philpott,	John	schoolmaster	Horsham	524	Chapter 6	1851
Pierce,	John	pauper of workhouse	West Grinsted	404	Chapter 12	1803
Pierce,	John	agricultural labourer	Horsham	639	Chapter 6	1830
Pledge,	Martha	-	?Horsham	412	Appendix	1804
Pledge,	Stephen	-	?Horsham	412	Appendix	1804
Pledge,	John	waiter	Horsham	412	Appendix	1804
Pollard,	Mr. John	farmer	Nuthurst	319	Chapter 9	1783
Pryne,	Mr.	attorney	?Leatherhead	418	Appendix	1805
Randall,	Mrs.	midwife	Kirdford	360	Chapter 1	1792
Read,	Henry	tramp	(no fixed abode)	509	Chapter 12	1845
Redford,	Mr.	farmer	Warnham	417	Chapter 1	1805
Richardson,	Daniel	Henry Murrell's apprentice	Horsham	425	Chapter 12	1808
Richardson,	-	uncle of William Stenning	Horsham	348	Chapter 2	1789
Robertson,	James	lawyer's clerk to Mr. Medwin	Horsham	419	Appendix	1809-1812
Robertson,	James	lawyer's clerk	Horsham	412	Appendix	1804
Robinson,	James	-	Shropshire	435	Chapter 3	1812
Rowland,	Sarah	?child	Horsham	364	Chapter 1	1794
Rowland,	Mr. Samuel	stone mason	Horsham	425	Chapter 12	1808
Sadler,	James	companion of James Booker	Horsham	507	Chapter 12	1841

Sadler,	Thomas	manservant at Warnham Court	Horsham	524	Chapter 6	1851
Sanctuary,	Mr.	magistrate	?Rusper	505	Chapter 9	1840
Sandham,	Mr. (William)	lawyer	Horsham	412	Appendix	1804
Sandham,	Mr. William	attorney at law	Horsham	412	Appendix	1804
Sandham,	Mr. (William)	farmer (?former lawyer or his son)	Horsham	452	Chapter 5	1818
Savage,	John	carpenter	Horsham	425	Chapter 12	1808
Scardefield,	William	?constable	?Horsham	348	Chapter 2	1789
Scutt,	John	servant of Mr. Agate	Storrington	505	Chapter 9	1840
Searle,	William	-	Horsham	412	Appendix	1804
Searle,	Thomas	friend of James Geere	Storrington	456	Chapter 6	1819
Sergison	Mr. Francis, senior	landowner	Cuckfield	336	Chapter 10	1787
Sergison,	Mr. Warden	eldest son and heir to Cuckfield Place	Cuckfield	336	Chapter 10	1777
Sergison,	Mr. Francis, junior	army officer	Cuckfield	336	Chapter 10	1777
Sharp,	Daniel	miller	Horsham	419	Appendix	1809-1812
Sharp,	-	constable	Horsham	348	Chapter 2	1789
Shine,	John	slater	Horsham	425	Chapter 12	1808
Smart,	Henry	farmer	Wisborough Green	360	Chapter 1	1792
Smith,	Mr. (William)	magistrate	Stopham	327	Chapter 12	1785
Smith,	Mr. William.	magistrate	Stopham	348	Chapter 2	1789
Smith,	Edward	young man	Horsham	639	Chapter 6	1830
Smithers,	William	labourer	Horsham	639	Chapter 6	1830
Snelling,	Francis	chemist	Horsham	504	Chapter 8	1840
Stanford,	Mr. William	wealthy farmer	West Grinsted	404	Chapter 12	1803
Stedman,	Mr. (William)	lawyer and magistrates' clerk	Horsham	510	Chapter 1	1845
Stedman,	Mr. William	magistrates' clerk	Horsham	492	Chapter 12	1833
Stedman,	Mr. William Smith	clerk to the magistrate's Bench	Horsham	509	Chapter 12	1845
Stedman,	Mr. (William)	magistrate's clerk	Horsham	507	Chapter 12	1841
Steer,	William	-	?Warnham	412	Appendix	1804
Stemp,	George	worked near Arundel	?	348	Chapter 2	1789
Stenning,	James (?senior)	labourer	Wisborough Green	360	Chapter 1	1792
Stenning,	Christopher	?labourer	?Wisborough Green	360	Chapter 1	1792
Stenning,	John	suspected thief	Wisborough Green	327	Chapter 12	1785
Stenning,	James junior	suspected thief	Wisborough Green	327	Chapter 12	1785
Stenning,	William	suspected thief	Wisborough Green	327	Chapter 12	1785
Stenning,	Greenfield	miller	Wisborough Green	327	Chapter 12	1785
Stenning,	Pat	father of John, James and William	Wisborough Green	327	Chapter 12	1785
Stenning,	William	unemployed	Wisborough Green	348	Chapter 2	1789
Stenning,	James	labourer and suspected thief	Wisborough Green	348	Chapter 2	1789
Stovell,	Steven	servant to Mr. William Lintott	Horsham	493	Chapter 12	1834
Stringer,	Mr. Richard	governor of workhouse	West Grinsted	404	Chapter 12	1803
Tasker,	William	-	Horsham	412	Appendix	1804
Taylor,	Edward (Ned)	-	?Horsham	412	Appendix	1804
Thomas,	Mr.	surgeon	Horsham	510	Chapter 1	1845
Thomas,	Mr. William Lanham	assistant overseer (of poor)	Horsham	492	Chapter 12	1833
Thorns,	Mrs. M.A.	lady who employed Mary Hall	Horsham	510	Chapter 1	1845
Thornton,	Richard	brewer, executor and trustee	Horsham	419	Appendix	1809-1812
Thornton,	Richard	schoolmaster	Horsham	343	Chapter 7	1788
Thorpe,	James	day labourer and poacher	Cuckfield	336	Chapter 10	1787
Tolhurst,	Mr.(John)	pawnbroker of West Street	Horsham	507	Chapter 12	1841
Tredcroft	Mr. (Nathaniel)	magistrate	Horsham	385	Chapter 12	1800
Tribe,	Mr.	magistates' clerk	Worthing	505	Chapter 9	1840
Tubb,	John	miller	West Grinsted	404	Chapter 12	1803
Tugwell,	John	boy	Horsham	508	Chapter 12	1843
Turner,	Henry	-	Storrington	456	Chapter 6	1819
Tyler,	John	?labourer	?Rusper	354	Chapter 1	1790
Tyler,	William	?labourer	?Rusper	354	Chapter 1	1790
Vaughan,	Henry	assistant sexton	Horsham	524	Chapter 6	1851
Vinall,	James	labourer	Horsham	343	Chapter 7	1788
Vowls,	Henry	hairdresser and barber	Horsham	504	Chapter 8	1840
Walder,	Mr.	?farmer	Washington	505	Chapter 9	1840
Walker,	Matthias	ironmonger	Horsham	508	Chapter 12	1843
Weller,	William	shopman	Horsham	493	Chapter 12	1834
Wells,	Mrs. (daughter)	companion of Sarah Floate	Storrington	505	Chapter 9	1840
West,	Thomas	labourer	Horsham /Rudgewick	394	Chapter 12	1801

Wheatland,	-	labourer	Washington	505	Chapter 9	1840
White,	William	miller	Pulborough	385	Chapter 12	1800
White,	Thomas	-	Storrington	456	Chapter 6	1819
Whitington,	John	servant of Mr. Walder	?Warminghurst	505	Chapter 9	1840
Whitman,	Nicholas	constable	Horsham	343	Chapter 7	1788
Whitmore,	Mr.	-	Horsham	452	Chapter 5	1818
Williard,	William	labourer	Shenfield, Essex	506	Chapter 12	1840
Williard,	Mary	farmer (Lower Bewbush)	Lower Beeding	506	Chapter 12	1840
Winch,	Joseph	guard of the Brighton and London van	?London	506	Chapter 12	1840
Wood,	Robert	farmer	Horsham	419	Appendix	1809-1812
Woodman,	Thomas	-	Horsham	639	Chapter 6	1830
Woolven,	Sarah	servant to Mr. Baker	Cowfold	509	Chapter 12	1845
Yohurst,	Charles	shop-boy	Horsham	493	Chapter 12	1834
Young.	Mr. Florance	executor of Thomas Cooper	?Leatherhead	418	Appendix	1805

List of cases

Cat. No.	Person or persons accused	Crime and date of trial
304	Edmund Drewitt Robert Drewitt	Theft from an Exciseman - 1777
307	William Evans	Riot in a Methodist Meeting - 1777
319	Thomas Ansell jun.	Attempted rape of Martha Baytupp - 1783
327	John Stenning James Stenning (The Younger) William Stenning	Theft of Pear Trees from the Rev. Morgan Evans - 1785
327 memo)	John Stenning	Theft of half a bushel of wheat from Mr Elliott - 1785
328	(not specified)	Defamation of the character of a lawyer by a schoolmaster - 1785
336	Francis Sergison Gent., John Kimber John Marchant	Riot, damage and threats - 1787
343	Richard Thornton	Tipping nightsoil on Gaol Green - 1788
348	William Stenning	Burglary of the shop of John Laker - 1789
354	James Chapman (The Younger) John Tyler William Tyler	Assault on William Markbee - 1790
360	James Stenning	Assault on John Older - 1792
360 (memo)	Christopher Stenning	Perjury - 1792
364	Frances Cooper	Assault on Sarah Marsh - 1794
375	Edward Bailey	Theft of 19 fowls from John Botting - 1796
385	John Boxall	Mill breaking and theft of flour - 1800
394	Thomas West	Theft of 11 duck eggs from George Brooke - 1801
404	Joseph Pierce	Theft of 10 ells of linen cloth from William Stanford - 1803
412	William Cooper	Dispute with Benjamin Boorer concerning the estate of John Boorer deceased - 1804
417	Dendy Napper	Assault on William Cooper - 1805
418	William Cooper	Dispute with the executors of Thomas Cooper - 1805
422	Ann Golding	Fraud and embezzlement of her master's money - 1806
425	John Shine	Theft of lead from Samuel Rowland and John Savage - 1808

429	Thomas Charles Medwin Stephen Dendy Richard Thornton	Case brought by Edmund Glyn concerning the estate of William Cooper, decd. - in Chancery, 1809-1812
435	John Hughes	Appeal against conviction for assisting escape of French prisoners - 1813
452	William Longhurst Daniel Harwood Thomas Philpot	Highway Robbery of Peter Dendy - 1818
456	James Geare	Manslaughter of Thomas Searle - 1819
492	Milford Mitchell	Theft of a gun from Philip Chasemore - 1833
493	Charles Oakes	Theft of tobacco from William Lintott - 1834
504	William Passell Henry Heath	Drugging drinks with 'Spanish Fly' - 1840
505	George Langley	Rape of Sarah Floate - 1840
506	Walter Williard (Nephew)	Theft of horse from Mary Williard (Widow) - 1840
507	James Booker James Sadler	Theft of Horse Roller and Spoon from Henry Padwick - 1841
508	George Charman	Theft of sovereigns from Mathias Walker - 1843
509	Thomas Coles Henry Read Peter Kensett	Theft of a copper from Richard Booker - 1845
510	Mary Hall (The Younger)	Attacking her mother with a knife - 1845
524	John Payne	Murder of William Gibson - 1851
639	Henry James Hewett	Murder of Edward Smith - 1830

Sources for the illustrations to be found in the text

Albery, William, *A Millennium of Facts on the History of Horsham and Sussex, 947-1947,* Horsham Museum Society, 1947.

Bain, Iain, *Thomas Bewick - an Illustrated record of his Life and Work*, published by the Laing Gallery, Tyne and Wear County Council Museums, 1979.

Bewick, Thomas, *My Life,* (first published 1862), edited by Iain Bain, Folio Society, 1981 (with illustrations).

Bowes and Carver, *Old English Cuts and Illustrations for Artists and Craftspeople,* Dover Publications Inc., New York, 1970. (This reproduces engravings published in London in the late 1780s and 1790s by the firm of Bowes and Carver).

Dickens, Charles, *Sketches by Boz,* with illustrations by George Cruikshank (first published in 1836).

Dudley, Howard, *The History and Antiquities of Horsham,* published in 1836.

Green, J.R., *A Short History of the English People,* illustrated edition, Macmillan and Co., 1894.

Harper, C.G., *The Brighton Road,* published in 1892.

Hurst, Dorothea, *Horsham: Its History and Antiquities,* first published anonymously in 1868.

Macmillan, Duncan, *Painting in Scotland - The Golden Age* (catalogue of 1986 exhibition).

Pyne, W.H., *Etchings of Rustic Figures for the embellishment of Landscape,* first published by Ackermann in 1814, republished by M. A. Nattali (copy in the Horsham Museum collections).

Pyne, W.H., *Microcosm, or a Picturesque Delineation of the Arts, Agriculture, Manufactures etc. of Great Britain -* republished by Luton Museum in booklets on *Early Trades and Industries* (1974) and *The Turnpike Age* (1970)

Trevelyan, G.M., *Illustrated English Social History* (the illustrated edition first published 1949-1952 in four volumes and later republished by Pelican Books in 1964).